Cardboard Modelling

A Manual of Cardboard Modelling,

With

Full Working Drawings and Instructions

By

William Heaton

Preface By T. G. Roper

With a New Foreword By Brittney McGann

©2019 Living Library Press

Living Library Press
Bristol, Virginia

This current edition is a reproduction of the original 1894 work published by O. NEWMANN & CO. of London, England. The current publisher has made minimal changes for the purpose of utilizing modern punctuation and numeration. American spellings have been used. All rights reserved. No part of this book may be reproduced without permission.

Table of Contents

Preface	1
Introduction	3
Foreword by Brittney McGann	6
Cardboard Modelling by William Heating	14
Notes on Models	32
Working Diagrams of the Models	38
Model No. 1 Triangular Key Label	38
Model No. 6 Book Cover	40
Model No. 7 Book Cover	42
Model No. 8 Puzzle Card Case	44
Model No. 9 Square Tray	46
Model No. 10 Square Tray	48
Model No. 11 Oblong Tray	50
Model No. 11a Oblong Tray	52
Model No. 12 Three Key Labels	54
Model No. 13 Portfolio	56
Model No. 14 Hexagonal Lamp Mat	58
Model No. 14a Hexagonal Tray	60
Model No. 15 Hexagonal Tray w/sloping sides	62
Model No. 16 Octagonal Lamp Mat	64
Model No. 17 Match Pocket	66
Model No. 18 Box with Lid	68
Model No. 19 Oblong Box w/hinge lid	70
Model No. 20 Needle Case	72
Model No. 21 Pocket Mirror	74
Model No. 22 Stationery Portfolio w/pocket	76
Model No. 23 Pen and Ink Tray	78
Model No. 24 Oblong Photo Frame	80
Model No. 25 Shaped Photo Frame	82
Model No. 26 Triangular Paper Weight	84
Model No. 27 Candle Screen	86
Model No. 28 Music Portfolio w/flaps	88
Model No. 29 Almanac Cover	90
Model No. 29a Draught Board	92
Model No. 30 Card Case w/pocket	94
Model No. 30a Pocket Case w/pencil slot	96

Model No. 31 Cubical Money Box	98
Model No. 32 (a, b, c, d) Four Silk Winders	100
Model No. 33 Circular Mat	102
Model No. 34 Twelve-Cornered Mat	104
Model No. 35 Square Tray w/rectangular divisions	106
Model No. 35a Square Tray w/diagonal divisions	118
Model No. 36 Pyramidal Watch Stand	110
Model No. 37 Oblong Tray w/sloping sides and projecting base	112
Model No. 38 Menu Tablet	114
Model No. 39 Wall Pocket	116
Model No. 40 Sliding Pen Box	118
Model No. 41 Cubical Box w/ hinge lid and double sides & lid	120
Model No. 42 Hexagonal Tray w/ sloping sides and curved edges	122
Model No. 43 Hexagonal Shelf or Wall Pocket	124
Model No. 44 Wall Pocket w/semi-circular front	126
Model No. 45 Irregular Octagonal Tray	128
Model No. 46 Irregular Octagonal Tray w/curved upper edges	130
Model No. 47 Oblong Tray w/curved edges	132
Model No. 48 Handkerchief Box w/double and projecting base & lid	134
Model No. 49 Toilet Mirror, Drawer, Slide, Mirror	136
Model No. 50 Stationery Cabinet	138
Model No. 51 Glove Box	140
Model No. 52 Box w/Hinge Lid	142
Model No. 53 Triangular Taper Holder	144
Model No. 54 Handkerchief Box w/lid	146
Model No. 55 Stationery Box	148
Appendix – Geometrical Models	150
Nos. 1-2	151
Nos. 3-4	152
Nos. 5-6	153
Nos. 7-8	154
Nos. 9-10	155
Nos. 11-12	156
Nos. 13-14	157
Nos. 15-16	158
Nos. 17-18	159
Nos. 19-20	160
Addenda	161

PREFACE

Is there such a thing as a general training for the muscles of the hand? Many are eagerly asking this question; and many, who are convinced that an affirmative answer must be given to it, are earnestly setting themselves to the task of devising courses of handwork for school children which will form a useful foundation for any craft which the scholar may subsequently practice in after-life.

In so far as handwork forms a branch of general education, it must not be merely mechanical, but should cooperate with literary work to strengthen and develop the intellectual powers. Mr. Heaton's series of exercises in Cardboard Work, which is based upon the practice in the Swedish schools, seems to fill a very definite place in any comprehensive scheme of manual training such as is intended to be co-extensive with the whole period of education.

The ordinary Kindergarten occupations, which afford preparatory training in the use of the hand for Infant Schools, can be carried on until the child is eight years old. Woodwork, whether Sloyd or some other form of it, can seldom be commenced with advantage before the age of eleven. Some kind of bridge, therefore, is required to cover this gap, and exercises in Cardboard seem to be admirably adapted for the purpose.

In working out any course of training for the hand, the points to be aimed at are that the exercises bring out accuracy in measuring and drawing, nicety in cutting out, and neatness in fitting together and finishing. Whoever is at the pains to cut out for himself even a few of Mr. Heaton's patterns quite correctly, will find out that he has carefully kept in view all the above points throughout his book. Experience shows that children of nine or ten years of age are interested in learning to make these models, and that, in the process, they become able to measure and draw out geometrical shapes with exactness, and to cut them out and fit them together with precision.

Mr. Heaton's course is arranged in accordance with the principles of Swedish Sloyd. Preliminary exercises are avoided. Some object is made at each lesson from the outset. In respect of difficulty, the exercises are graded with great care. Each model forms an introduction to the following one, and is an advance upon the one which has been completed just before.

Children who have outgrown Kindergarten occupations will find in the execution of Mr. Heaton's series of Cardboard Models an agreeable exercise and a sound training for hand and eye.

T. G. ROOPER

INTRODUCTION

THIS Manual is issued in deference to a very pronounced and general demand for a definite course of work in *Cardboard Modelling* on Sloyd lines. The need for working drawings has been seriously felt in connection with the Bradford Classes, and it is hoped that these Drawings and Accompanying Directions may be of service to teachers who may not possess a set of Models, from which their pupils may work directly.

It may be more appropriate to make a few general observations here rather than in the body of the book.

The nature of the work is such that average Standard II children may reasonably be expected to begin it.

The teaching should be, as a rule, in the earlier stages, from the blackboard. The drawing and setting out of the plans proves, at first, a stumbling block with very young children; but patient blackboard work will overcome this. The unequal progress of the children may prove an impediment in the way of this collective teaching. When this stage is reached, the Sloyd principle of individual teaching comes into operation with advantage.

The earlier faults in cutting are mainly due to the children being unable to keep the metal square firmly in position while the successive cuts are made. This is not to be wondered at, seeing how difficult it is at first to get children to draw straight lines by aid of a ruler. As a matter of fact, the attention becomes so concentrated upon the work the knife is doing, that the children overlook the duty imposed upon the left hand—of holding the square firmly to the line of cutting. Rigid accuracy, either in cutting or binding, should not, in the working of the earlier models, be insisted upon. If the teacher is satisfied that the work has been done to the best of the pupil's ability, it would be unwise to insist upon too many repetitions of the exercise. This would tend to breed a distaste for the work. The degree of accuracy demanded should be heightened as the pupils proceed and become more familiar with the operations.

Economy in the use of material should be attended to from the beginning. I have seen adults, when left to themselves, cut out a small model from near the center of a large sheet of cardboard. This is done from want of thought. The model required could as easily have been obtained from near the corner of the sheet, leaving a large and unimpaired surface for succeeding models. If the drawing is placed near the edge of the sheet, the pupils should be taught to cut straight through to the edge. I have found that the tendency is for them to cut out a model, leaving cardboard all round the vacant space. This impairs the accuracy of the cutting at the angles of the figures.

Approximate English measures are given with a view to simplifying the demands made upon young pupils. At the same time, the adoption of the Metric measurements is strongly advised. At a time when teachers and representative business bodies are pressing forward in the direction of the adoption of the sensible Metric system, the introduction of Metric measurements should not be lightly regarded.

The basis of measurement generally adopted is that of 1 c. = 3/8 in. English. In some cases an apparent discrepancy may occur. Where the Metric measure of a model involves fifths—e.g. 1.5 c., 12.5 c., etc.—the unit of calculation is 5 c. = 2 in. The English measures given are really only approximate, and have, as far as possible, been adapted to the varying requirements of the models. The difference occurring in larger measures becomes evident, because the margin between the actual Metric measure and the approximate English measure of 1 c. = 3/8 in. becomes multiplied in the larger measurements. Thus 1 c. = 3/8 in. approximately, though not quite, and 10 c. = 4 in. (nearly); but the difference between the actual and the approximate is magnified in increasing the measures. If 1 c. = 3/8 in., then 9 c. should equal 3 3/8 in.; but, as a matter of fact,

9 c. = 3½ in., while 10 c. equal, not 3¾ in., but 3 15/16 in. This slight margin between the two measurements has been mainly disregarded, and, where measurements in the Metric System give multiples of 5, the 5 c. = 2 in. base has been adopted; and, where measures which did not lend themselves readily to English rule are given, the base of 1 c. = 3/8 in. has been taken, because eighths are marked on ordinary English rules.

The use of pencil compasses is recommended to insure accuracy of measurement.

The room in which cardboard work is carried on should be lighted from the right of the pupils as they are at work, as all the cutting is done on that side of the square, and the slightest shadow thrown across the line of cutting leads to uncertainty and inaccuracy.

Children should not be kept continuously at work for lengthened periods—the recommendation as to intervals of smart physical exercises should be put in practice, or the work will become tiresome and of ill effect.

The models from which the drawings are taken are the work of Swedish children. Can there be any doubt as to the ability of English children to do similar work?

BRADFORD,

March, 1893

FOREWORD by Brittney McGann

On May 17, 2017, I made the most expensive book purchase in my life. For months, I had been searching the Charlotte Mason archives for references to books about cardboard sloyd. I only ever saw one book mentioned. It was a book that was scheduled throughout all the years of available programmes from Mason's lifetime. Since I saw no other cardboard sloyd book in the programmes, I concluded that it must be the best. I decided I had to locate and study it. The book was extremely difficult to find, but after a few months of searching, I was finally able to secure a copy of *A Manual of Cardboard Modelling* by William Heaton. I was delighted to find that Mr. T.G. Rooper, PNEU supporter and friend of Miss Mason, had written the preface.

Mr. Heaton's book on cardboard sloyd is a continuation of a progressive course of Sloyd and the culmination of its benefits. Mr. Devonshire explains: "It should be clearly understood that it is Card-board Sloyd that is considered essential for the full development of the child." (1905, p.8). One might say that sloyd is incomplete if it ends with paper. It needs to progress to cardboard. That is why I am so happy to offer a new introduction to this book, which has been forgotten for too long. It is my hope that through this book, cardboard sloyd will once again become an essential part of a wide and generous curriculum.

In his article entitled "Harmonious Relations Between Physical Training and Handicrafts," J.W. Devonshire gives a basic progression for cardboard sloyd lessons:

> To each child is given a thin piece of card-board, a sloyd knife, a ruler marked off into centimeters, and a strip of glued binding. After a few essays in cutting and binding the child begins simple models, such as mats, key labels and other flat articles, which by gradual progression lead on to slip covers, boxes, portfolios, photograph frames, and eventually to bookbinding. (Devonshire, 1905, p. 8)

This is exactly the order given by Mr. Heaton. That is one of the many reasons I believe that his book set the standard for cardboard sloyd in the PNEU. Mrs. Steinthal praises Heaton's book, and cites an interesting passage in which Heaton quotes Rousseau:

> I would press teachers very earnestly to study Mr. Heaton's book, which is so carefully prepared that any adult could work the models without any previous training, and then teach it to her pupils… Rousseau preferred that Emile learnt to build highways rather than make flowers or porcelain. He says, "Let us choose a respectable trade, but let us ever remember that there is no respectability without utility." Mr. Heaton maintains and proves that, "cardboard work is a

step, and a good step, in this direction." It specially helps to form habits of order, exactness, neatness and cleanliness, and forms a bridge over which the boy passes to Sloyd at the age of eleven or twelve. (Steinthal, 1894, p. 925)

In her article "Cardboard Sloyd," Miss Pennethorne gives three categories of benefits that result if sloyd is used to "its fullest educational value": physical, mental and moral. Though written over one hundred years ago, teachers today can expect to see the same benefits manifested in their students. Let's explore each category in turn, using Miss Pennethorne's framework. She lists the physical benefits as follows:

1. It trains the eye to accuracy (accuracy being understood as absolute, not relative) in (a) drawing a straight line, (b) measuring distances and angles, (c) cutting on the line drawn.

2. It trains the hand to follow the guidance of the eye, and to obey exactly the impulse of the motor nerves transmitting the message of what the hand is required to do.

3. It strengthens the muscles of the hand by exercise. (Pennethorne, 1906, p. 3)

A child in Form 1a, about 7 years old, begins using the knife for paper sloyd, training his hand to accuracy and meticulous control, and following the judgments made through the eye. The student learns to control different muscles for different results in the same way that he might control different large muscles in his body. These controlled movements allow him to become the master of his tools. I have found several references to links between Swedish Drill (developing control of specific muscles of the body) and sloyd (developing control in specific muscles of the hand), and the two working together for optimum physical benefit:

This fact is recognized in the teaching of Swedish drill by the best methods, in which the pupil is told which special muscles each exercise is intended to develop, and so he can concentrate his thought on those particular muscles, thus gaining the fullest possible benefit from the exercise. (Pennethorne, 1906, p.6)

It may be said that a perfect system of handicrafts tends to increase and refine on individual lines the powers of mind and body already developed by a perfect system of gymnastics. We can see how the finger stretching and clasping paves the way for the individual use of the ten fingers, when binding or gluing a Sloyd model. The nerve and decision gained in the grasping and suspension movements help in the mastery and use of tools; while wrist exercises considerably ease the sweeping movements so often needed in wood-carving. (Devonshire, 1905, p. 9)

That same intentional movement increases the student's powers in drawing specifically so that he might make accurate representations of what he sees. This power is what brings us to the second category, the mental benefits. Mr. Russell, who I believe introduced the PNEU to the philosophy of sloyd, shows plainly the link between right work and right thinking:

> The simple straight line is the very basis of all construction, and enters, in its various combinations, into nearly everything our hands can fashion—and yet how few of us can even draw it on paper, much less produce it in wood! We are satisfied with an approximation, with getting it nearly right. And is not that the characteristic of most of our thought, our action—that we are satisfied if we can keep pretty close to the line of the ideal? But must not the boy who learns to cut accurately learn to think accurately? Is it not thought that guides the knife? (Russell, 1893, p. 328)

In The Parents' Review article "The Value of Art Training & Manual Work," Mrs. Steinthal concurs that sloyd develops thinking skills that are as important as the manual skills. She says that manual training:

> …conveys to the mind that it is to impart power and skill to the hand; but it is not altogether so. Power and skill of hand are much, but not everything. The eye has to take in information, of which the mind forms a mental picture, and, guided by practical experience, it selects what is needed. The mind seeks to express in the concrete the picture it has formed. It is, in fact, training in thought by other means than verbal language. Its aims are those which are, or should be, the aims of all general education, the acquisition of knowledge and development of power. It has therefore a right to a place in education. Hand work is not introduced in home and school teaching as technical instruction in its strict sense. (Steinthal, 1897, p.414)

So not only does the practice of sloyd develop the ability to think rightly and control the use of our hands, but it also aids in the use of the imagination. The student will learn to imagine a three-dimensional object from a two-dimensional diagram and then learn to draw a two-dimensional diagram from a three-dimensional model. By combining reasoning abilities, imagination, and mental control with manual dexterity, the student will grow in his ability to make and do what is necessary, a skill which will be useful throughout life, both personally and professionally.

The student can also take these mental powers into other areas of his schooling. His reasoning powers and measuring skills apply to math. He becomes better at nature journaling because of his increased ability to make his hand draw what his eye sees. He takes pride in his Book of Centuries because he can accurately reproduce artifacts of interest on his page. He has an understanding of the foundation of architecture and the confidence that comes from accomplishments made by his own power. Mr. Devonshire calls that confidence "moral progress" (1905, p. 9), which leads to the final benefit that can be expected from diligent lessons in sloyd.

This area of moral benefit is the one I least expected when I began my research several years ago, but it is the one that I believe to be the most important. During his presentation to the Woodward branch of the PNEU, Mr. Russell asks hypothetically what children would learn if they were educated on sloyd alone. He says:

> … they would certainly train their eyes to real power in seeing, and their hands to real power in doing, and … be sure at least of a sound body. But that is not all. They would be doing something too towards a sound mind… they would learn… to be orderly, accurate, attentive, industrious, thoughtful, and self-reliant—nay, I will go even further, and add truthful. Orderliness, accuracy, attention, industry, thoughtfulness, self-reliance, truthfulness—verily a list of nearly all the virtues! (Russell, 1893, p. 328)

But this "moral progress" doesn't apply to the student alone; it also applies to his relations with people outside of himself. Russell puts the idea well in this lengthy quote:

> You will be giving them a fuller understanding, and therefore a fuller pleasure, in some of the commoner everyday things of life, and in the underlying principles of innumerable human productions; but, above all—and sometimes, when I look about me, I think that this gain alone should suffice to give Slöjd an honorable place in our schools—you will, if your methods are sound, and your own heart is right, give them respect and love for all honest hand-work and honest hand-workers, and so save them from that blight of shame which still fastens on many and many a human being at the thought of doing any honest work whatever, and on still more perhaps at the thought of working with their hands!

> Ladies and Gentlemen, you must pardon me for saying in this connection that, in my opinion, one of the first steps towards making this world a happier place is to get men and women not only to say but to believe—and belief is practice—that no work that is essential to the continuance and well-being of humanity is below the dignity of the best or wisest of us, and further, that all work that is unpleasant, or repulsive, or involves danger, must, within certain obvious limits, and in the absence of perfected machinery, be shared unshirkingly by all. (Russell, 1893, pp. 332-333)

In this idea, I see an illustration of the Christian body:

> Don't think you are better than you really are. Be honest in your evaluation of yourselves, measuring yourselves by the faith God has given us. Just as our bodies have many parts and each part has a special function, so it is with Christ's body. We are many parts of one body, and we all belong to each other. In his grace, God has given us different gifts for doing certain things well. (NLT, 2013, Romans 12:3b-6)

Craftsmanship has long been stigmatized and it is simply wrong to perpetuate this idea that educated people don't get their hands dirty. There is dignity in every dirty job and every kind of rough work. It may be that the child's best way to serve is in some honest handwork. College is not the best direction for every student, and introducing handwork (especially sloyd) offers a chance to find a different route. Continuing from Russell's earlier quote, he says:

> But you will be doing more than this. You will be affording them an opportunity of showing, before it is too late, where their special powers lie—in the head or in the hand—and helping them to find an answer to that fateful question—that chance too often mis-answers for us—What shall I do with my life? (Russell, 1893, p. 332)

The benefits of sloyd are well worth the effort. It's even worth any accidental drops of blood that might be necessary to remedy carelessness! It has been my great pleasure to study how sloyd was taught by the Parents' Union School, and I hope it will be a joy to Charlotte Mason teachers and students to have this excellent book by William Heaton available once again. I will close this section with a little stanza written by the students at Scale How, showing the lighter side (and difficulty) of training in sloyd:

> Do you want to study
> What sloyd and carton mean?
> Be a Scale How student,
> On models you'll get keen,
> Just use your knife quite freely,
> And cut your finger so,
> Here is scope for genius
> And works like hang! dash! blow! (PNEU, 1916, p. 9)

Notes on Cardboard Sloyd Lessons

Before a child begins this course in cardboard sloyd, he should have experience in paper folding (origami) and should have practiced paper sloyd for at least one year (or preferably two). I consider Paper Modelling, written by M. Swannell and republished by Living Library Press, to be the best starting course.

In Form 2, handicrafts move from morning lessons to afternoon occupations. By this time, the student should already have control over his knife and skill in accurately measuring and cutting, but these lessons are still not handed over to the child without adult supervision and oversight. In the previous quote from Mrs. Steinthal, we see that she recommends that the teacher study the book herself and learn how to do the models, then teach the students. If the student has a solid foundation in paper sloyd, and the teacher has taken the time to ensure that the new skills are understood, then the student will soon be ready to do models completely on his own; the teacher will only need to be on hand for questions and difficulties.

Students were expected to complete four perfectly executed models per term during Form 2 (grades four through six). The first models are key labels, followed by mats, book covers, trays, and boxes. Students would have been doing each model more than once before being allowed to move on to the next project. However, the child should not be required to do the same model so many times that he becomes discouraged. Lessons were still short (20-30 minutes), and several new skills were introduced in this form, causing the student to work more slowly and more carefully compared to the previous year's work. The new skills include:

Transitioning to the metric system for increased accuracy when increasing or decreasing the size of the model.

Using thicker paper and learning the appropriate amount of pressure to score it without cutting through.

How to bind edges with bookbinding tape.

So, while the initial models seem quite simple, students are building up the skills which will allow them to be successful with the more complicated models.

Forms 3 and 4 continue along the same lines as Form 2, but doing six models per term. Models increase in difficulty because of the more complicated geometric shapes used in the diagrams. We do not know if sloyd was done in every term. If it was, models from Heaton's book would be exhausted by the second year of Form 3, but we can see it scheduled in Form 4 as well. Because of that, I think it is likely that sloyd was omitted from some terms in Forms 3 and 4.

The last skill to be mastered in cardboard sloyd, before moving on to wood sloyd or bookbinding, was the ability to draw a diagram from a geometric model: converting a three-dimensional object to a two-dimensional drawing. Plans for these models, to be made by the teacher, are included in the appendix of William Heaton's book.

Some of the language and terms used by Mr. Heaton are not commonly used today, so I have included some explanations and tips as a basic update.

The "cardboard" used for cardboard sloyd is simply thick cardstock. A variety of thicknesses can be used, including thin chipboard, like the type used for retail gift boxes. Thicker than that is not recommended. My preferred cardstock is 110 lb (300 g/m2); it is readily available in craft stores and comes in a variety of different colors.

The same craft knife (with fresh blades) used for paper sloyd can be used for cardboard, but if wood sloyd is the goal for the student, it may be worth purchasing an actual sloyd knife and learning how to sharpen and care for the knife. I remind the reader that both types of knives are quite sharp and, while I do allow my own children in Forms 1 and 2 to wield them, I always ensure that the knives are put away and kept out of reach when lessons are over.

For binding we have many more options than the students would have had a hundred years ago. In addition to bookbinding tape (which didn't always come "pre-gummed" in Mason's day), we have washi tape, in many patterns and widths, as well as colorful duct tape and masking tape. It is perfectly fine to take some liberties here with the choice of materials. Bookbinding tape can be quite expensive and, if used at all, can be reserved for special projects once more proficiency has been gained. The other kinds of tape are much less expensive and are readily available at most craft stores.

References:

Devonshire, J. (1905). Harmonious Relations Between Physical Training & Handicrafts. *L'Umile Pianta*, March, 1905 (pp. 8-11). London: Parents' National Educational Union.

NLT. (2013). *Holy Bible: New Living Translation*. Carol Stream, IL: Tyndale House Publishers.

Pennethorne, R. (1906). Cardboard Sloyd. *L'Umile Pianta*, April, 1906 (pp. 3-6). London: Parents' National Educational Union.

PNEU. (1916). Dear Ex-Students. *L'Umile Pianta*, November, 1916 (pp. 8-11). London: Parents' National Educational Union.

Russell, C. (1893). On Some Aspects of Slöjd. *The Parents' Review*, volume 4 (pp. 321-333). London: Parents' National Educational Union.

Steinthal (1894). Aunt Mai's Budget. *The Parents' Review*, volume 4 (pp. 922-931). London: Parents' National Educational Union.

Steinthal (1897). The Value of Art Training & Manual Work. *The Parents' Review*, volume 8 (pp. 414-418). London: Parents' National Educational Union.

CARDBOARD MODELLING

BY WILLIAM HEATON (BRADFORD)

There is a general demand for the introduction of some form of manual training into Elementary Schools, and the circular issued by the Science and Art Department in 1890 is significant. It is not a part of my purpose to discuss the relative merits of the various systems of manual training which are being urged upon the attention of teachers and educationalists generally. Each system has its claims, and, to many, the necessity for the adoption, in the near future, of some scheme of work must be apparent.

Along with this prevalent demand for the inclusion of manual work in the school curriculum there is a feeling that some preparatory work should be taken which should continue the Kindergarten training of the infant schools, and lead up to, and be an introduction to, the woodwork generally regarded as being fitted for the upper standards. Much has been done of late years for the development of the "doing" faculty of the infant-school children, and rightly so—the results amply justify the attention given to this branch of educational work. Very much is proposed for the upper standard children, and school managers and teachers are alike alive to the needs of the times. And yet but little has been suggested for filling up the gap between the close of infant-school life and the introduction of the children to the heavier work of their later school career. It is a serious break in the continuity of the process of faculty training which occurs when a child leaves the happy hunting-ground of the infant school and is introduced into the first of those matter-of-fact standards. The early and concluding portions of the scholar's school life are being provided for; the middle distance has received scant attention. It must be a great loss to stop this training at the age of six and to discontinue it for five or six years, knowing that in the last few years the child will be expected to undertake work altogether distinct from the ordinary school course. If a good system is to be built up, the foundation must be made more secure, and the intermediate preparation made continuous and thorough. The circular referred to recognizes this fact, for among the "suggestions" contained in it is this: "It is desirable to practice children in cutting out and putting together solid models in paper or cardboard." It is my purpose to follow up this "suggestion" by introducing to my readers a workable scheme capable of adaption to the needs and powers of the younger children in our schools. Cardboard work is a part of the general system of Sloyd, though the orthodox Sloyder is not enthusiastic on some of its features.

The tests, to which different classes of work proposed for children must be subjected in order to estimate their value as means of training, are numerous and searching. Cardboard work, when put to these orthodox tests, will, as we shall see, fall short in some respects of a perfectly ideal course. And yet the extent to which it has been introduced into Continental schools would seem to show that it has a real and practical value. Its adoption in the schools of Sweden is established and general. In France, both the Elementary and Intermediate schools include it in their courses of work; in the former being confined to cutting cardboard into geometric forms, while in the latter it is extended to the making of objects—along with basket making, clay modeling, wire and wood work. In various parts of Germany the manual course includes basket work, brush making, wood carving, and cardboard work. At Leipzig, cardboard work is a special feature, while one of the recommendations of the Belgian Department of Education in 1883 was that cardboard modeling should be taken for three hours per week by pupils from eight to ten years of age. In Vienna this class of work is in operation.

There is evidence on all hands of attempts to bridge over the gap of three or four years of school life, before the introduction of the heavier forms of manual work would be regarded as desirable, by some such work as this. Various schemes are offered for lower standard children—*e.g.* straw plaiting, clay modeling, etc. Of none of these is it for me to speak disparagingly. At the same time, our ordinary text-books on manual work contain such meager details of cardboard work that its merits as an educational method have not attracted much attention, while most of them agree in saying that such work is suitable for the lower standards.

When we consider the age of the children for whose use this work is suggested, it will be seen that too much ought not to be expected. The work itself must serve the purposes laid down by one authority, viz.:

> 1. To strengthen the body, to invigorate the constitution of the child, to place the child in hygienic conditions favorable to general physical development.

> 2. To give him at an early age the qualities of readiness, quickness, and manual dexterity—that promptness and certainty of moment which, while most valuable to everyone, is especially necessary for such pupils as are destined for some manual profession.

To put this cardboard work to the crucial tests to which all forms of manual training ought to be put, those of the Naas authorities, will show that in most respects it is of very great value. I say that all such schemes ought to be put to these tests, because they are tests suggested by many years of experience and experiment, and only those systems which will to a considerable extent stand the ordeal of submission to them should be regarded as suitable for the occupation of our school children. In answering the questions suggested as being so comprehensive and searching, the answers "can only have a relative, not a positive value, as they must be considered in the light of special circumstances, and also of experience in actual work." This is Herr Salomon's reservation, and is applicable to an inquiry into any form of manual work. Now as to cardboard work:

1. Is it framed according to the capabilities of children? —The Naas answer is "Yes and No" (more "Yes" than "No"—the "Yes" coming first). This answer seems to be somewhat indefinite, and requires to be more plainly stated. Models may be presented in a series which would indubitably demand the negative answer, as being beyond the capability of average children. Experience alone would enable us to adequately elaborate such a course of models and exercises as should fully deserve the affirmative reply, and be regarded as being "according to the capabilities of the children." I have the assurance of many experts in this branch of educational work that the series of models I propose to give are of such a character as to remove many objections to cardboard modelling, and that the models are such as may unhesitatingly be regarded as fulfilling the requirements of the question.

The principal difficulty lies in the inability of very young children to successfully execute the necessary geometrical constructions, and to do the finishing work neatly. But actual experience among English children in Sloyd work and carpentry tends to remove any doubt, for young boys in many cases are much more dexterous than adults, and more than theorists give them credit for being. Their fingers are more supple and less clumsy. Given work which they can comprehend, the exercises in which, while involving new work, contain no extraordinary demands upon their powers, and there is no doubt of the ability of young children to tackle it with creditable success. The result of recent experiments with Bradford schoolboys in Sloyd work is amply satisfactory on this point.

2. Does it excite and sustain interest? —The answer usually given is a doubtful "Yes," the doubt being dependent upon the class of models and the nature of exercises involved. The course is not of a cast-iron nature—it is capable of adaptation to the varying needs and tastes of pupils or localities. It is for the teacher to make the work fit the time or the place. Given a rational gradation of models and exercises, in which the pupils see a gradually accumulating store of objects worthy of their care, and in the construction of which much valuable training has been obtained, even if thinly veiled by the knack of the teacher, the interest cannot fail to be aroused and sustained. This is an important feature. In the ordinary subjects there is little to excite interest, and very little incentive to continued effort. Motive is lacking, and the child studies mainly

because he is compelled. Manual training—and cardboard modelling not less than other forms—attracts and pleases the child because it here finds food for the imperious need of activity which inheres in the nature of its being; it also sees in it the results of its efforts, and can appreciate and enjoy them. Manual training has a greater educational value than that which is purely intellectual.

3. An unequivocally favorable feature of this work is that the articles made, and the result of the work generally, will be found to be serviceable. There are two considerations involved here—(i.) the objects, (ii.) the tendency of the work. Sloyd work admits of no objects as models which have not a serviceable value, and in the execution of which the necessary work involved has not a substantial educational value. Objects of luxury and ornamentation are not admissible. Toys and objects conducive to pleasure alone are not regarded as fit models to engage the attention of young workers who are to be trained to respect both work and the workman, and to whom toys give but a passing pleasure. The making of a toy yields no more pleasure to a child than the making of an object which may be of service to himself or at home, and the additional pleasure realized on the completion of a useful article acts as a powerful stimulus to renewed effort. The general throwing over of toy-making in Swedish schools is evidence of the value set both by parents and children upon exercises involving the making of articles of utility. At the same time, this utilitarian character of the objects to be made is a secondary consideration, the essence of the question being as to the training involved in the execution of the models. This matter is discussed later on. Still, given on one hand a set of toy models, the making of which gives valuable exercises in the training of the faculties, and, on the other hand, a series of useful articles for models—articles which in themselves have a use apart from the mere making, and the completion of which necessitates exercise having equal value from an educational point of view—the latter will be the more acceptable series for our purpose. So that if the series I suggest can be shown to approach the nature of the second series suggested above, it should meet with the readier acceptance. Among the objects included are lamp-mats, needle-cases, wall watch-pockets, boxes of various kinds, portfolios, etc., each and all of practical service, while requiring a gradually increasing facility in manipulation.

This demand for utility in the articles to be made is on a par with the too-little-recognized principle of compelling children, for the sake of the training and as a resource in times of failure in other directions, to learn some useful occupation. Rousseau wished Emile to learn a trade—not that of an embroiderer, a gilder, or varnisher—he preferred that he should build highways rather than make flowers on porcelain. So he says, "Let us choose a respectable trade, but let us ever remember that there is no respectability without utility." Cardboard work is a step, and a good step, in this direction.

4. One of the chief aims of all manual training in schools should be to inculcate a respect for rough work. This, from the nature of the work, our special work cannot, perhaps, be said to do. Every type of manual training should tend to the breaking down of the foolish prejudice against rough and hard work, which has flooded the labor market with clerks and with inefficient teachers and professional men. Cardboard modelling may possibly be considered too "finnicking" to do this, if taken throughout the standards. Applied to the three or four lower standards, it will serve as a preparation for the further course of work with tools adapted for the upper standards. It may be safely taken for granted that, by a course of cardboard modelling, the hand and eye will have received a fine training before the stage at which rough work would commence, and hence more rapid progress would result when this stage is reached. The reservation as to actual experience would be necessary here; but the extent to which cardboard work is taken in Continental schools points to the inference that such work has been found useful as a preparation for the tool-work practiced by the older children.

5. Work of this character is an admirable training in habits of order and exactness. At the same time that we are bringing children to regard work with the hands with respect, we must also, by the introduction of finer work, begin to inculcate habits of the nature named—so shall these habits tell upon the future work of the pupils. The exercises involved in this neat binding of accurately-cut figures demand careful and exact eye and finger work.

6. Rightly used, cardboard modelling may be made eminently instrumental in teaching habits of neatness and cleanliness. In Continental schools the binding is cut in strips and the gumming is left to the pupils. This latter, without very great care, cannot be done without the young children smearing themselves and their work. The danger of this is reduced to a minimum by the introduction of strips which are ready gummed—the moistening and fixing alone being left for the children to do. Even in these circumstances carelessness will result in untidy work, as in many other branches of an ordinary school course. Surely a good object has been achieved if otherwise dirty work has been rendered capable of achievement in a cleanly fashion. Dirty work has to be done, and a step in the right direction has been taken if a habit of doing such dirty work with the least possible amount of smearing and untidiness has been formed.

7. Does it cultivate a sense of form? To this query, a doubtful affirmative is usually given in reply, the doubt being as to whether the sense of form is fully cultivated by the production of figures which are only capable of geometrical construction, and those mainly, if not entirely, composed of straight lines. This is a serious question and one involving one of the main considerations to be taken into account in discussing any scheme of work. "In manual work the construction of objects should tend to develop the aesthetic feeling by their pure forms." Every useful object may be made beautiful by

the adoption of pure forms in its construction, and in the arrangement of a set of models we must look first to their usefulness as objects, coupled with the value of the training their construction imparts; but we must give to these same objects the most elegant forms possible.

Naturally most of the objects in a set of cardboard models must be constructed on straight-line forms, owing to the difficulty which may be expected in the production of symmetrical curved forms by young children. Yet curved lines are freely introduced of such a nature as to be well within the capability of young children. An ordinary square or oblong tray may have its upper edges curved or scalloped in simple fashion, while the backs of wall-pockets or portfolios may be varied in curve and design as necessity may demand.

8. One very serious objection may be fairly urged. Unless the lessons are very short, and followed by physical exercises carefully arranged so as to counteract the ill effects of the stooping posture necessarily adopted by pupils for the production of cardboard models, positive injury may be done to the muscles of the chest and back. In this case our work would be unworthy of the name of education, for the physical well-being of our pupils must have a foremost place in our consideration. But the same charge may, with very great reason, be urged against a very large proportion of our ordinary school work. The stooping over desks for writing, etc., the twisted positions too commonly adopted by children, and too often left unchecked, are themselves a considerable item in the arguments brought forward by promoters of manual training against a too exclusive system of intellectual school work. The gravamen of the charge has been considerably reduced by the almost universal adoption of physical exercises in schools; and it is in this direction we must look for the antidote to the ill effects which may be anticipated for pupils in cardboard work. Any unhealthy tendency may be checked by the conscientious observance of two or three minutes spent in smart physical exercises for every fifteen or twenty minutes of cramping work.

9. Any good system of manual training must present a course of work allowing of methodical arrangement; by this being meant that its exercises and models may be classified in such a manner as to fulfill the dictum that progress shall be easy, and that no great step shall intervene between one exercise and another.

This condition our course of work amply fulfills.

10. Manual dexterity is one of the objects aimed at in all Sloyd work. There are two classes of manual dexterity—(1) General; (2) Particular.

General manual dexterity is such as would enable a pupil to attempt manual work of any kind, with greater readiness than if he had received no preliminary manual training. Particular manual dexterity is the result of the training of one particular or special organ or set of functions.

Cardboard work can claim a position midway between these two, for while the actual training of the physical powers may be limited to the cultivation of dexterity in the fingers and hand, it is a distinct aid in the development of the faculties of observation, neatness, and nicety of touch.

Having briefly considered the questions of the position and utility of cardboard work, it remains to describe the materials required and the method of working, and to give a course of suggestive models.

MATERIALS

The materials required are not numerous, and may be obtained at reasonable prices.

Cardboard

This material is usually of a buff or yellowish brown color, and of a firm and strong texture. Various thicknesses may be obtained, but for children's use it is not advisable to have a very stout board. A medium board which is not of a soft pulpy nature will be suitable. Few models, if any, need to be made of very thick board; and even for the use of adults a medium board will suffice. The essential feature of a good cardboard is that, being cut half or three parts through, it may be bent backward from the cut without fraying or creasing the surface of the board in the neighborhood of the bend. The Bradford Cardboard Sloyd Company supplies two thicknesses, one having one hundred, and the other eighty, sheets to the hundredweight. The former is amply strong enough for all practical purposes, and is, if anything, too firm and too difficult to cut for very young children. The price is from *12/6* to *15/-* per hundredweight. Messrs O. Newmann & Co. keep an abundant assortment of different cardboards in stock, and their prices are equally reasonable.

Work need not, and in fact should not, be confined to boards of one uniform tint. Variety of coloring will lend interest to the work, and exercise a good influence on the artistic taste of the pupils. Thinner sheets of plain board may be used, and covered with colored and pattern papers at a small additional cost. This covering should be done by machine in order that the fancy paper may adhere firmly and evenly, and not "rough up" when cut. The publishers display a beautiful set of plain, colored, fancy, and pattern papers, which are extremely artistic in finish and reasonable in price, and they undertake to cover plain boards with any paper selected by the purchaser for a small charge over and above the cost of boards and paper. The pretty effect obtained is more than commensurate with the small sum charged for the covering.

Cloth Binding

The binding usually adopted is bookbinders' cloth, which may be obtained in sheets ready gummed, or specially prepared—cut in strips and gummed ready for use. Both sheets and strips will be needed. In Sweden, the cloth is not previously gummed and cut, the pupils having to prepare the binding for themselves. The supply of ready-prepared binding reduces the danger of the pupils rendering themselves or their work dirty. Cloth of various colors may be obtained. For the boards mentioned, of a buff or yellowish brown color, black or red cloth has been found serviceable. The cloth is supplied in sheets 18 inches square, at 5d per sheet, or cut into strips 18 inches long and 3/8 inches wide, ready for use at 2s per 100. A black cloth of a neat twilled pattern has been found very serviceable for binding edges, with cloth of a bolder pattern for corners, or for covering spaces of any extent. Colored cloth to match any shade of paper can be obtained from the publishers of this Manual.

Paper Binding

Paper binding may also be used, and, though not so strong as the cloth, adheres neatly and firmly. It may be had in sheets, ungummed, at 1s 6d. per quire; or, specially prepared and gummed, cut into strips for edging, 20 inches long at 1s per 100. Morocco paper and smooth enamel paper are both useful for covering insides of book covers, etc., as also, when cut into strips of a good width, for covering-in the unbound edges of pieces of cardboard, which are joined at some distance apart by a wide strip of cloth, forming a hinge, as in a book cover or the flap of a portfolio. Price is as given above, and various patterns and colors may be obtained.

The Knife

Various patterns of knives are used for this class of work. They vary in strength and shape, two features which must have prominence in selecting a good knife for this purpose.

FIG. 1

Figure 1 represents a knife which has been used for some time in the Bradford Cardboard Classes and was the outcome of much experimenting and many trials. It is supplied at 5s or 5s 6d per dozen, with rosewood handles. The curved cutting edge is its distinguishing characteristic, giving it an advantage over the German knife (Fig. 2), which cuts only with the point. The curved cutting edge prepares the way for the final cut of the point, and helps to keep the cut straight. Later experience has shown that this knife is not perfect. The curve is too flat and does not allow of the hand being held in the best position for exerting the necessary amount of force. The tendency with its use is to cut with the point, the extreme flatness of the curve not allowing the hand to be held sufficiently high.

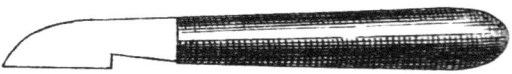

FIG. 2

The German knife (Fig. 2) appears to be very unsuitable for the purpose for which it is intended. Cutting with the point, unless it is very sharp indeed, tends to tear the face of the board, and gives facility for the cut to diverge from the line. It is well made and costs ninepence.

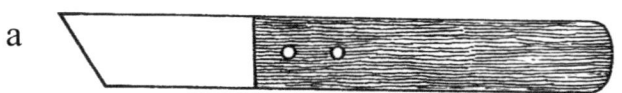

FIG 3.

The London School Board Knife (Fig. 3) is specially made for that Board. It is a strong substantial knife, well adapted for its purpose. The blade is short and thick, tapering to a fine cutting edge at *a*, and is firmly riveted into the cocoa handle.

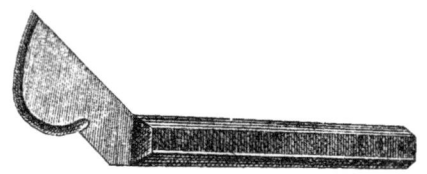

This knife was designed by an Inspector of Schools to overcome the difficulty commonly experienced in cutting a hard pressed board. The necessary force and pressure is obtained in a natural manner by its use, the shape allowing the hand to be held well up. It sells at 8s per dozen.

*The Leipzig Cardboard Knife is a copy of the one in use at the Leipzig Manual Training School. It is a well-made knife with a short firm blade and rosewood handle, nicely shaped for a firm grasp. The blade is firmly riveted half the length of the handle. The shape of the blade is a compromise between No. 1 and No. 2, the cutting point being midway between the two long sides of the blade. It is a knife well adapted for its purpose, and is sold at six shillings per dozen.

FIG 4

* Messrs. Newmann & Co. have now brought out this eminently serviceable knife, known as the O.N. knife, made of good Sheffield steel in England, and its extremely reasonable price places it within the reach of teachers requiring a large number. The price is 5s per dozen.

a

FIG.5

This is an admirable shaped knife for cardboard work. The angle of the cutting edge, *a*, lends itself well to the use to which it is to be put. With a sharp-pointed knife the tendency is to cut with the point alone. A child holds it at a most convenient angle for cutting. It is made of cast-steel. The tang goes through the handle, and is riveted, giving additional strength. It is furnished with a brass cap and supplied with a rosewood handle. It can be obtained at about eightpence or tenpence.

Straw Boards

are useful for covering the desks or tables upon which the work is performed. Cut to the width required, and fastened down with drawing pins, they form an excellent protection to the surface of the desk, while capable of easy removal or refitting, in case the desk should be required for ordinary purposes. They last a long time with care, and, being cheap—6d or 9d per large sheet—their renewal is a matter of slight expense.

Squares

The squares used for drawing and for cutting must be of metal, otherwise the edges may be cut and the angle distorted. They may be of iron, 12 inches each arm, stamped with the usual measures (at 1*s* each), or an excellent brass set square at 1s 2d may be preferred. The former are liable to rust, and need care and attention if they are to be kept in a fit state for use, or they will dirty and disfigure the work.

Flat rulers, ordinary pencil compasses, and a supply of hard drawing pencils will be needed.

Accessories

There are several other things the possession of which, while not absolutely essential, may prove of service. Scissors with fine points are useful in fitting binding into corners; bone folders, something like the ordinary pocket paper knife, are of service for pressing down the binding, so as to make it adhere firmly and evenly; while sponges, of the usual scholars' type, may prevent a too liberal use of the natural secretion for moistening purposes. (Some of the models have small tape-holes punched in them, and for this purpose a small steel punch should be procured.) Le Page's or Knight's liquid glue should be at hand in case some of the binding proves recalcitrant and refuses to adhere, while the procuring of a small steel square (9d or 1s) is recommended for the purpose of testing the accuracy of the cutting and fitting.

METHOD OF WORKING

The actual work may be roughly but conveniently divided into three parts: (1) drawing, (2) cutting, (3) binding.

1. The drawing of the model on the cardboard should be exact, and taken from actual measurement of the models, from a scale drawing, or, with young children, from a blackboard drawing. Even young children may fairly be expected to draw plans of most of the models, and work from them on to the cardboard. The lines should be fine but distinct, as the cutting has to be very exact.

2. Cutting—This is an important part of the work, the finish and exactness of the model depending materially upon the accuracy of the cutting. Practice alone will enable a pupil, whether a child or adult, to cut with ease, certainty, and accuracy. The figure having been drawn on the cardboard, place the edge of the metal square close along the line of cutting. Hold the knife firmly in the clenched hand, and draw the cutting edge gently, but firmly, along the line. Slope the knife slightly towards the body so as to facilitate the running of the blade along the board, and to take advantage of the curved cutting edge. Let the first stroke of the knife be gentle, and repeat the strokes again and again, increasing the force and pressure at each repetition. If the first stroke is heavy and forced, it will be almost impossible to keep to the line. The object is to secure a cut edge exactly perpendicular to the face of the board, and unjagged; otherwise the binding will lap over unevenly, or, where the cut edge has to form a join, as at the corner of a box or tray, the junction will be uneven and inexact. This knack of accurate cutting is not given even to every adult at a first attempt. I know of one lady who made half-a-dozen attempts to cut out the first model, and failed—failed ingloriously—through lack of attention to the points named, i.e. graduation of force in cutting, and attention to perpendicular edge, with just a suspicion of weakness in the left hand in keeping the metal square firmly in its place. When it is remembered that exactness of work is one of the main objects aimed at, it will be realized how important it is to cultivate a good style of cutting. In many of the models, as in trays, boxes, etc., where the object is made out of one piece of cardboard, the cutting is to be but half-way through the board—and the pupil will soon learn to know by the "feel" when he has cut sufficiently deep to allow of the board being bent backward without fraying or creasing the material. In all cutting operations it is essential to keep a firm wrist, and a sharp eye on the cutting line and perpendicular edge.

3. Binding—This part of the work may, without due care, tend to be dirty and sticky. I will take one of the earlier models as an example—the square key label. Having cut out the figure, take one of the strips of binding and double

longitudinally for a distance about equal to the edge to be bound; place it along the edge of the square and cut off to exact length, and double it carefully and exactly. Fit it to the edge of the square, and see that the binding overlaps equally on both faces; open out the binding and moisten with damp sponge or otherwise, in either case taking care that the moistening is of the nature of "dabbing," so as not to wipe off the gum. Now place the binding carefully along one edge of the square, fitting one side only, after making sure that the two faces are equally overlapped. Bring over the other half and press gently with the fingers to the face of the board, taking care that the binding adheres evenly along the whole of the cut edge. Now use the bone folder to press out any wrinkles caused by air bubbles, and, by passing the folder or thumb nail firmly along the cut edge, see that the binding adheres firmly, and that no folds are made. The least inequality along the cut edge will result in pressure, forcing out the binding along the face of the board. These wrinkles and inequalities must be gently worked out by pressure of the thumb and finger till the whole of the binding along both faces and edge is evenly and firmly affixed.

Bind the first edge straight from end to end; the second and succeeding edges should be fitted so as to join or overlap diagonally, the last strip of a figure being fitted at both ends. The fitting is easily effected by gentle pressure of the knife from corner to edge of binding along the diagonal line, the part loosened thereby being cut off either with the knife or scissors. The binding of a square appears thus (Fig. 6):

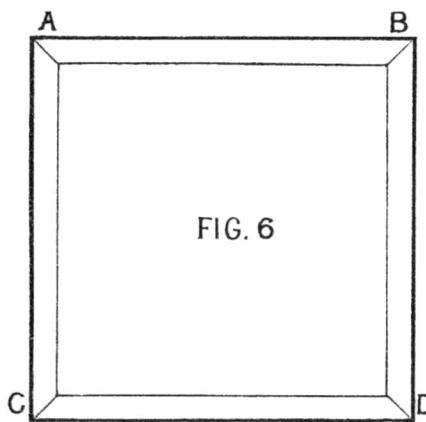

FIG. 6

(1) *AB* bound end to end.

(2) *BC* fitted at *B*, straight edge at *C*.

(3) *AD* fitted at *A*, straight at *D*.

(4) *DC* fitted along diagonals at *D* and *C*.

A little practice will enable pupils to bind straight edges with facility and accuracy, and the earlier models give abundant exercise in this work.

In some of the models, as in portfolios, book covers, etc. binding, as for hinges, has to be affixed. Wider strips should be cut from the sheets for these. By accurately measuring the width of the strips cut, and the space to be left between the two pieces of board, the amount of overlapping on each sheet may be accurately ruled off. Few difficulties are presented, and to a pupil who has mastered the art of neat and accurate binding in the earlier models, progress will be easy and natural.

SERIES OF MODELS

The following is given as a reliable and graduated series of models. The measures given are in centimeters. The sizes stated are not arbitrarily fixed. Teachers may modify to suit circumstances, but when once a definite size or measurement has been fixed upon, it is essential that work done upon that model shall be accurate and exact. It is not essential that the metric measurements be adhered to, though this is strongly recommended. The measurements may be adapted to English needs by remembering that a centimeter is about 3/8 inches of English measure, or, more exactly, 5 centimeters = 2 inches.

LIST OF MODELS

No.	Description	Metric Measure			English Measure		
		c.	c.	c.	in.	in.	in.
1.	Triangular Key Label	8	0	0	3 1/8	0	0
2.	Rectangular Key Label	8	5	0	3 1/8	2	0
3.	Square Key Label	6	6	0	2 3/8	2 3/8	0
4.	Oblong Table Mat	10	8	0	4	3 1/8	0
5.	Square Table Mat	15	15	0	5 7/8	5 7/8	0
5a.	Oblong Table Mat	21	17	0	8 ¼	6 ¾	0
5b.	Square Table Mat	20	20	0	7 7/8	7 7/8	0

		Metric Measure			English Measure		
No.	Description	c.	c.	c.	in.	in.	in.
6.	Book Cover	17	13	0	6 ¾	5 1/8	0
7.	Book Cover, cloth corners	22	18	0	8 ¾	7 1/8	0
8.	Puzzle Card Case	10	6	0	4	2 3/8	0
9.	Square Tray, perpendicular sides	10	10	2	4	4	¾
10.	Square Tray, sloping sides	9	9	3	3 ½	3 ½	1 3/16
11.	Oblong Tray, sloping sides	18	8	3	7 1/8	3 1/8	1 3/16
11*a*.	Oblong Tray, sloping sides	20	5	3	7 7/8	2	1 3/16
12.	Key Labels (*a*) Rhombus	5	5	0	2	2	0
	(*b*) Rhomboid	6	5	0	2 3/8	2	0
	(*c*) Trapezoid	6	5	4	2 3/8	2	1 5/8
13.	Portfolio	23	18	0	9	7 1/8	0
14.	Hexagonal Lamp Mat	8	radius	0	3 1/8	radius	0
14*a*.	Hexagonal Tray, perpendicular sides	9	6	3	3 ½	2 3/8	1 1/8
15.	Hexagonal Tray, sloping sides	9	6	3.5	3 ½	2 3/8	1 3/8
16.	Octagonal Lamp Mat	8	radius	0	3 1/8	radius	0
17.	Match Pocket	14	9	0	5 ½	3 ½	0
18.	Oblong Box, with lid	9	6	3	3 ½	2 3/8	1 3/16

		Metric Measure			English Measure		
No.	Description	c.	c.	c.	in.	in.	in.
19.	Oblong Box, with hinged lid	10	7	3.5	4	2 ¾	1 3/8
20.	Needle Case	8	5	0	3 1/8	2	0
21.	Pocket Mirror	9	5.5	0	3 ½	2 1/8	0
22.	Portfolio, with pocket	23	18	0	9	7 1/8	0
23.	Pen and Ink Tray	21	11	4	8 1/4	4 3/8	1 5/8
24.	Photo Frame	20.5	16.5	0	8 1/8	6 ½	0
25.	Shaped Photo Frame	16	13	0	6 ¼	5 1/8	0
26.	Triangular Paper Weight	11	11	15.5	4 3/8	4 3/8	6 1/8
27.	Candle Screen	28	12	0	11	4 ¾	0
28.	Music Portfolio	35	25	0	13 7/8	9 7/8	0
29.	Almanac Cover	11.5	10	0	4 ½	4	0
29*a*.	Draught Board	26	26	0	10 ¼	10 ¼	0
30.	Card Case, with pocket	11	7	0	4 3/8	2 ¾	0
30*a*	Pocket Case, with pencil slot	21	9	0	8 ¼	3 ½	0
31.	Cubical Money Box	7	7	7	2 ¾	2 ¾	2 ¾
32.	Silk Winders	4	0	0	1 5/8	0	0
	" " (*a*)	6	5	0	2 3/8	2	0

		Metric Measure			English Measure		
No.	Description	c.	c.	c.	in.	in.	in.
	" " (b)	6	5	0	2 3/8	2	0
	" " (c)	5.5	0	0	2 3/16	0	0
33.	Circular Mat	6	radius	0	2 3/8	radius	0
34.	Twelve-Cornered Mat	10	radius	0	4	radius	0
35.	Square Tray, with cross divisions	10	10	2	4	4	¾
35a.	Square Tray, with diagonal divisions	9	9	3	3 ½	3 ½	1 ¼
36.	Pyramidal Watch Stand	16	12	0	6 ¼	4 ¾	0
37.	Oblong Tray, with sloping sides and projecting base	12.5	10	3	5	4	1 1/8
38.	Menu Tablet	17	12	0	6 ¾	4 ¾	0
39.	Wall Pocket	26	20	0	10 ¼	7 ¾	0
40.	Sliding Pen Box	20	5.5	3	8	2 ¼	1 ¼
41.	Cubical Box, with hinged lid	6	6	6	2 3/8	2 3/8	2 3/8
42.	Hexagonal Tray	10	4	0	4	1 5/8	0
43.	Hexagonal Shelf	17	7	11	6 5/8	2 ¾	4 3/8
44.	Semi-circular Shelf	14.5	6.5	5	7 ½	2 9/16	2
45.	Octagonal Tray	9	9	3	3 ½	3 ½	1 3/16
46.	Octagonal Tray, curved edges	9	9	3	3 ½	3 ½	1 3/16

		Metric Measure			English Measure		
No.	Description	c.	c.	c.	in.	in.	in.
47.	Oblong Tray, curved edges	18	8	3	7 1/4	3	1 1/8
48.	Handkerchief Box	15	15	7	5 7/8	5 7/8	2 ¾
49.	Toilet Mirror, with drawer	14	9	3	5 ½	3 ½	1 3/16
50.	Stationery Cabinet	16	14	6	6 ¼	5 ½	2 3/8
51.	Glove Box	28	8	3	11	3 1/8	1 3/16
52.	Oblong Box, with hinged lid	16	10	7.5	6 ¼	4	3
53.	Triangular Taper Box	16	9	7.5	6 ¼	3 ½	3
54.	Handkerchief Box, separate lid	17	14	5	6 5/8	5 ½	2
55.	Stationery Box, with hinged lid and falling front	20	12.5	6.5	7 7/8	4 7/8	2 9/16

NOTES ON THE MODELS

Models 1-5b afford exercises of gradually increasing difficulty, and at the same time give good notions of form. The gradations in length of cutting and binding are necessary to ensure accuracy and neatness.

Some teachers may prefer to take Model No. 3 first, and Model No. 1 in its place.

Models 6 and 7 begin the allocation to actual objects, and possibly will be the first to arouse enthusiasm.

Model No. 8 is a somewhat difficult model, its construction being intricate. If the familiar clothes-horse hinge is kept in mind, the difficulty may be to some extent lessened.

Models 9, 10, 11, 12 begin the really useful articles, and much interest will be aroused in their construction. They are applications of the work done in earlier models. The cutting out of the corners and triangular pieces for forming slope should be particularly neat and clean, so that the corners may fit exactly.

Model No. 12, involving three different geometrical figures, is an exercise in binding various angles. The whole may readily be worked out of one strip of board, if the cutting is even and the edges are perpendicular to faces.

Model No. 13 is a continuation of Models 6 and 7, with an added flap, requiring additional care in adjusting, and neatness of work.

Models 14-16 include further knowledge of geometric forms, and increased difficulty of drawing, cutting-out, and fitting. The further demands made upon the ability to bind awkward angles and to fit neatly are considerable, but progressive in character.

Model 17 is an involved and lengthy exercise in drawing, binding, and fitting. The cutting must be very exact, or the match tray will be out of shape and fit badly.

Models 18 and 19 continue exercises in previous models (11 and 11*a*), with the addition of details which lend additional interest to their construction.

Model 20 is an extension of the work in Models 6, 7, including the covering of the faces of the boards as distinct from the binding of the edges. The addition of a gimped oblong of flannel, kept in by a string of silk or fancy cord tied in a bow, will complete the model.

Model 21 is a very pretty model, requiring care and neatness in construction. Mirrors of the size required may be obtained at a cheap rate from the glass firms.

Model 22 is a further development of Models 7 and 13. The main difficulty lies in the construction of the pocket.

Model 23 is a useful and interest-inspiring example of cardboard work. The drawing and cutting should be very exact. The addition of inner skeleton squares to the side spaces would materially strengthen the whole.

Models 24, 25 are amplified examples of rectangular models, and tend to draw out the faculty of inventiveness. They illustrate the adaptation of the ordinary rectangular forms, with ready additions, to the construction of objects of household use. Their completion leads to ideas of home decoration. They are a step in the direction of a training of the taste.

Model 26 involves perfect examples of the need for exactness in measuring, drawing, cutting, and fitting. Good fish glue should be used in joining the four triangles. The extra width of the binding brings in an additional exercise. Exact fitting at corners and the angular joins of the binding form additional points of interest.

Model 27 —The drawing of one fold of the screen is given—the other two are similar. The central fold has holes punched on each long side. Join the three folds by silk ribbon tied in bows. This model adds to the interest, while involving a combination of the rectangular and triangular figures.

Model 28 enlarges upon the work given in Nos. 6, 7, 13, 22, by the adoption of larger measurements and the addition of flaps with similar hinge joining. A useful model, the construction of which implies proficiency in cutting and binding of extra length. The series arrives at its longest cuts and bindings in these exercises.

Model 29 —An extension of Model 20, involving similar exercises on a larger scale.

Model 29a returns to the square, with the addition of exercises involving accuracy in drawing and cutting-out of smaller squares. The main point in this model is accuracy.

Model 30 yields additional exercise in cutting-out and fitting of the pocket. It is not an easy model—its completion necessitates thought and care. It is an example of a model which is of personal use.

Model 30a gives additional interest to No. 30 by the addition of the pencil slot. It is an exaggerated copy of No. 20. A further model may be made with one or two pockets formed as in No. 30.

Model 31 returns to the square, with the addition of combination of similar figures. Additional exercises are included in the punching of the holes and the cutting of the slit.

Model 32—Four interesting geometrical figures, giving additional interest in "form" and development of "figure," and extra exercises in binding angles.

Model 33—An entirely new figure—introduces curves for cutting and binding. If the binding is stretched while moist, the curve will be neatly bound. This is better than cutting out and fitting at intervals. The covering of the faces should be of different colors. Taste is cultivated.

Model 34—An apparently difficult figure, but easy, if directions are followed. Gives further training in "form," and in binding angles.

Model 35 returns, in the main, to Model 9, with additional practice in cutting divisions. Care must be taken to cut the upper part of one division and the lower part of the other. Many models are spoiled by cutting the upper or lower part of both strips. Adds interest to the model, and gives exercise in fitting and gluing.

Model 35a—Similar to 35. Care must be taken to measure diagonal of upper angles and base for the two long sides of each strip. Involves exercises in accuracy of measurement, fitting, and gluing.

Model 36—In some series placed much earlier in the models. A continuation of 1 and 17. A difficult model, involving care in fitting. Start with an equilateral base, and isosceles sides. Main difficulty is in fitting the circular watch-ring. Bind the rim and cover insides with a contrasting-colored cloth or paper. Over the notch in rim add a small screw hook, previously backing with an extra piece of cardboard or wood, as a stay.

Model 37—An extension of No. 11, with more minute measurements. Addition of projecting base serves to strengthen the model, and to revise previous exercises. Gives a lesson in utility. Models 10, 11, and 11a were good; but 37 is stronger and more serviceable.

Model 38 involves once more long cuts with an idea of design. It will be necessary to cut out and fit the binding of the circular corners; as the arcs are short and stretching, the binding may not be sufficient to fit neatly. Writing tablets may be readily obtained of local dealers in glassware.

Model 39—An intricate model. Divides itself into two parts: (1) the back, (2) front of pocket. The construction of the back should be attended to first. This may appear to be difficult, but the distances given are symmetrical, and not much difficulty should be experienced in setting out the drawing. The open front should be cut out neatly. Stout blue or other colored paper should be used for forming body of pocket.

Model 40 continues exercises of previous Models 11, 11a, 18, and 19. In drawing out figure for tray, exact measurements must be used. For the cover, allowance should be made for the thickness of the cardboard in use. The measures given are for cardboard of rather more than average thickness. The binding of the ends of the cover forms a new exercise.

Model 41 is an enlargement of Model No. 31, by the addition of a hinged lid, with a tag, and double sides. The inner sides are drawn on similar lines to the box itself, allowance being made for the thickness of the cardboard. Like No. 40, this is a usable model, and lends extra interest.

Model 42 introduces curves, and involves somewhat intricate drawing. It is a pretty model, yielding a recapitulation of previous models, with added interest as an ornamental and useful article.

Model 43 introduces a new feature—the addition of a separate slip, fitted by half cuts—and necessitates great care in fitting and binding. Home decoration is again prominent, and utility gives interest to the work.

Model 44—The fitting of a separate slip by bending is another stage in the development of designing and manipulation.

Model 45 is a deferred development of No. 16, necessitating more care and deftness than could be expected when the child had reached No. 16. Calls for extreme accuracy in minute measurements and finish in drawing, cutting, and fitting.

Model 46 is an advance on No. 45, by the addition of curves. The measurements are minute, and should be very exact if angles are to fit.

Model 47 returns to the oblong as the fundamental construction, and grafts curves on to this early figure. The setting-out may appear somewhat intricate. Attend first to the distances which set off the base, then the distances which give the sloping corners, and last of all the measurements for the freehand curves. A pretty model, involving in the actual fitting and binding no more than some of the previous oblong models, but providing a neat and ornamental object of household service.

Model 48 is an elaboration of Model 5, with the addition of a few accessories. The lid should be held in a perpendicular position when fitting the restraining tape. The double lid and base are additions to Model 19.

Model 49 divides itself into three parts—(1) drawer, (2) slide for drawer, (3) mirror—with the addition of a drawer front and a base for the slide of the same size as the completed mirror. Begin with the drawer, which is another form of No. 11, with perpendicular sides and the addition of a front projecting beyond the sides. Then draw slide according to plan, allowing for the thickness of the board. The construction of the mirror is exactly on the lines of that in Model 21, the dimensions being greater.

Model 50 is a combination of the rectangular forms practiced in the early models to form an article of daily use. The back, sides, base and front are obtained from one piece of cardboard. The partitions are separate, and fixed in with a touch of glue. They are kept firmly in position by the addition of the strips obtained in Direction 13 (Model 50), which should be cut to the measure of the cabinet, allowance being made for the thickness of the cardboard of the partition slips.

The additional models inserted in the list, and distinguished by letters, have been added for the purpose of affording additional practice in cutting and binding, especially in the earlier part of the course.

Models 29a, 30a, and 35a give additional exercises, similar in character to those involved in earlier models, and are at the same time objects of practical use.

Supplementary models have been added, which are mostly modifications of other models in the series, and are suggestive of further additions which may be made by teachers.

Drawings for the construction of a set of Models, for use in school, are given as an Appendix.

WORKING DIAGRAMS OF THE MODELS

MODEL No. 1

TRIANGULAR KEY LABEL

8 c. (3 1/8 in)

1. Describe an equilateral triangle of 8 c. (3 1/8 in.)

2. Cut out with clean perpendicular edge.

3. Bind whole side from *A* to *C*, cutting off the ends in a line with *AB* and *BC*.

4. Bind *AB*, fitting along diagonal *Aa*, and cut off in line with edge *BC*.

5. Bind *BC*, fitting along diagonals *Bb* and *Cc*.

6. A small hole should be punched in one of the angles.

MODELS Nos. 2, 3, 4, 5, 5*a*, 5*b*

KEY LABELS and TABLE MATS do not require further drawings than that given in Figure 6 in the text.

See List of Models for dimensions.

CARDBOARD MODELLING

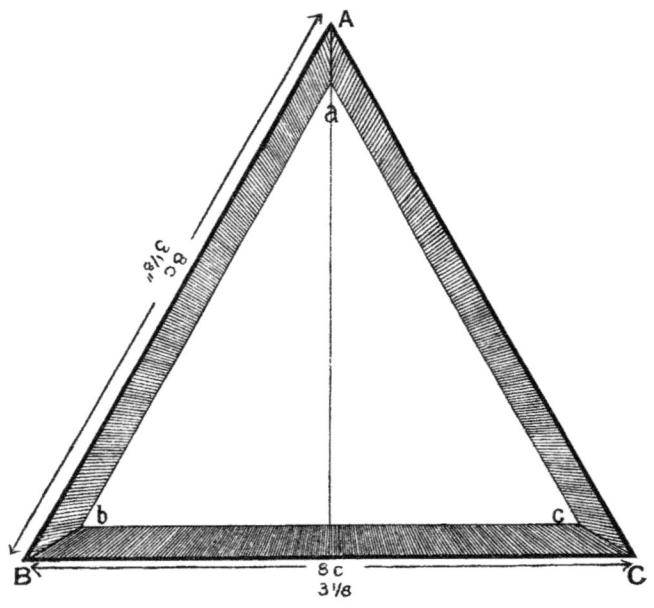

Full size of Model

MODEL No. 6

BOOK COVER

17c. x 13 c. (6 ¾ in. x 5 1/8 in.)

1. Cut two oblongs, each 17 c. x 13 c. (6 ¾ in. x 5 1/8 in.)

2. Bind two 13 c. edges and one 17 c. edge of each.

3. Cut a strip of cloth, 19 c. x 5 c. (7 ½ in. x 2 in.)

4. Join the two oblongs by this strip, leaving 1 c. (3/8 in.) between them, and allowing the hinge strip to overlap 1 c. (3/8 in.) at each end. This is most easily done by drawing lines *ab* and *cd* 2 c. (3/4 in.) from the unbound edges, and fitting the hinge strip to the lines.

5. Cut a strip of enamel paper, 16 ½ c. x 5 c. (6 ½ in. x 2 in.); rule lines on opposite sides of oblongs similar to *ab*, *cd*. Lay the cover open on the bench, fit the gummed strip of paper along *ab* and *cd*, and thus cover in all raw edges.

CARDBOARD MODELLING

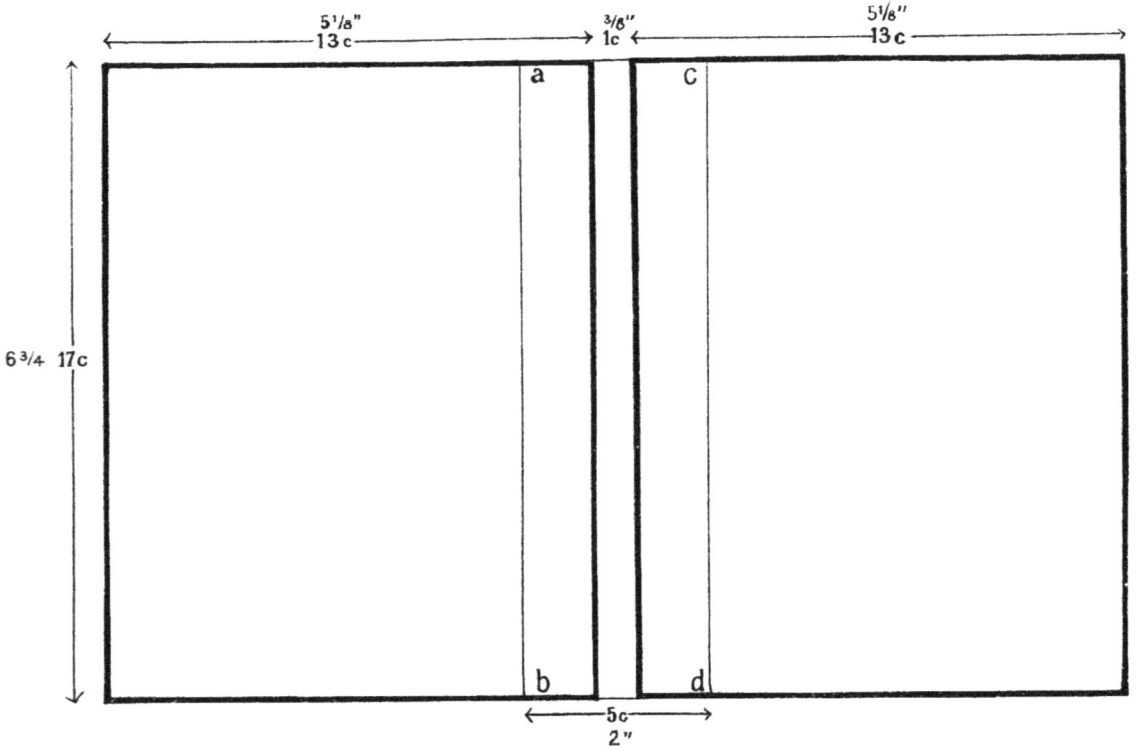

Half size of Model

MODEL No. 7

BOOK COVER—with cloth corners

22 c. X 18 c. (8 ¾ in. x 7 1/8 in.)

1. Cut out two oblongs of cardboard, each 22 c. x 18 c. (8 ¾ in. x 7 1/8 in.)

2. Set off 5 c. (2 in.) along each side from angles *A, B, C, D*.

3. Cut out four triangles of cloth, base 9 c. (3 ½ in.), sides 6 c. (2 3/8 in.)

4. Draw lines across each angle, as from *a* to *b*.

5. Bind the corners by placing the 9 c. base of each cloth triangle along each line drawn in Direction No. 4 and folding sides over the inside 1 c. from each edge, cutting out so as to fit along the diagonal lines as in Models 1 to 5*b*.

6. Cut a strip of cloth 24 c. x 5 c. (9 1/2 in x 2 in.); draw lines *cd, ef* 2 centimeters (3/4 in.) from each unbound inner edge of oblongs.

7. Bind this strip along *cd, ef*, so as to leave 1 c. (3/8 in.) between the two oblongs of cardboard—the ends of the strip to fold over to inside 1 c. at each end.

8. Cut a strip of enamel paper and fix evenly over the inner face of hinge joining.

The dotted lines show the outside appearance of the corner bindings.

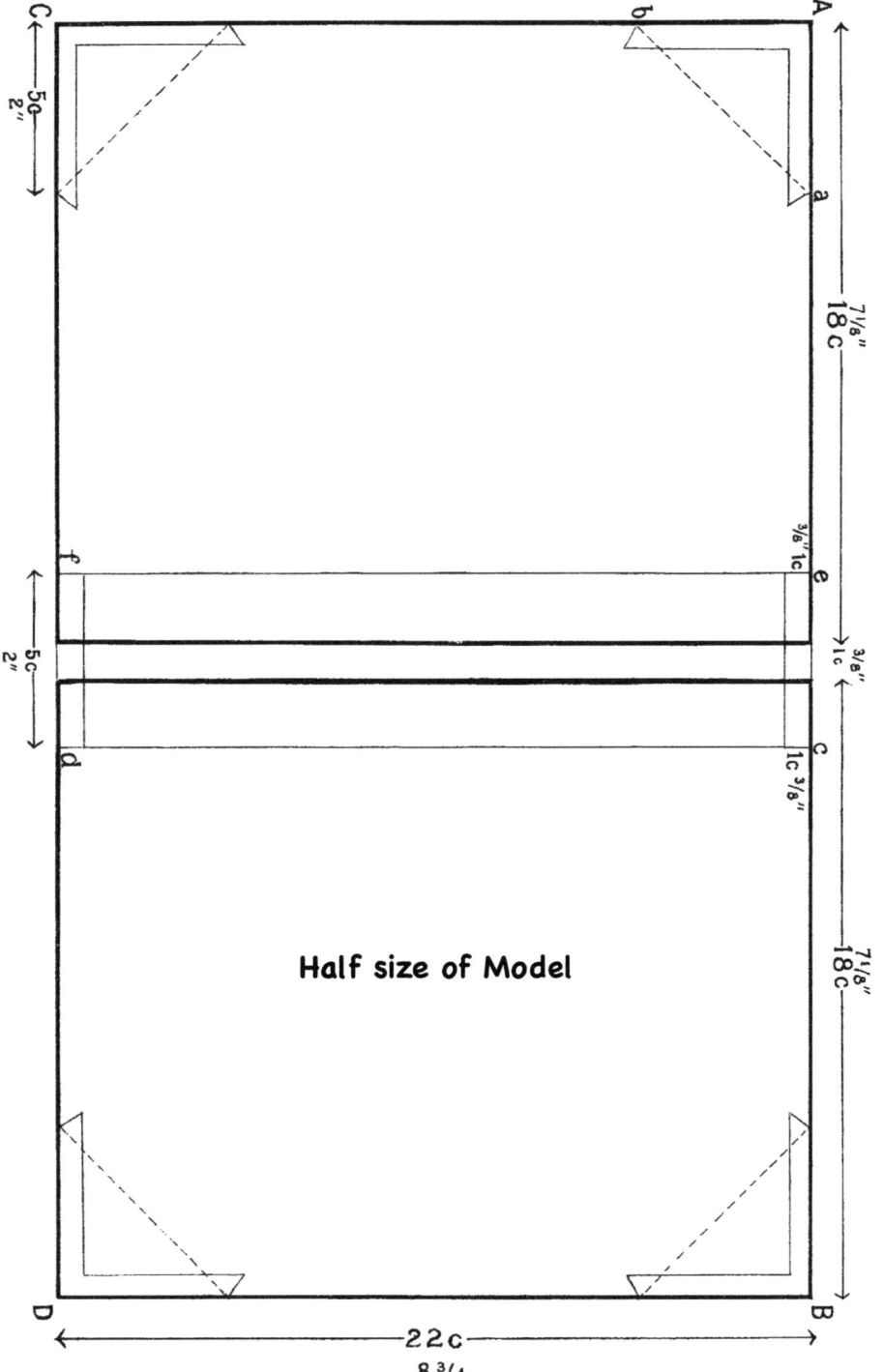

Half size of Model

43

MODEL No. 8

PUZZLE CARD CASE

10 c. X 6 c. (4 in. x 2 3/8 in.)

1. Cut out four oblongs, each 10 c. x 6 c. (4 in. x 2 3/8 in.), as *A*, *B*, *a*, *b*.

2. Bind *A* and *B* as in Model No. 2; leave *a* and *b* unbound.

3. To *a* gum two strips of narrow colored silk ribbon 1 ½ c. (5/8 in.) from each end. To *b* (as in Figure *b*) gum silk strips 3 c. (1 1/8 in.) from each end.

4. Fold these lengths of ribbon away from the faces to which they are gummed, and across the other faces. Bring *a* and *b* close together, and fasten the loose ends of each silk ribbon on the other oblong. Thus, take ribbon *1* across the opposite face of *a* and attach as at *1a*; strip *2* across the opposite face of *a* and attach at *2a*; strip *3* across the opposite face of oblong *b* and attach to oblong *a* at *3a*; and strip *4* across the other face of *b* and attach at *4a* to oblong *a*. Before fastening the strips bring the two oblongs close together and pull the strips tight.

5. Take oblongs *A* and *B,* and glue securely, edge to edge, to oblongs *a* and *b*, so as to cover all the gummed end of ribbon. Leave the whole for a time under heavy pressure to secure even adherence.

This is a difficult model, in which the preliminary operations are closely allied to those involved in the early models; the difficulty is in fitting. The characteristic clothes-horse hinge will show itself immediately the model is completed. It forms a pretty puzzle or card-case capable of being opened from either side. Fig. *C* shows the inner appearance of the model when completed.

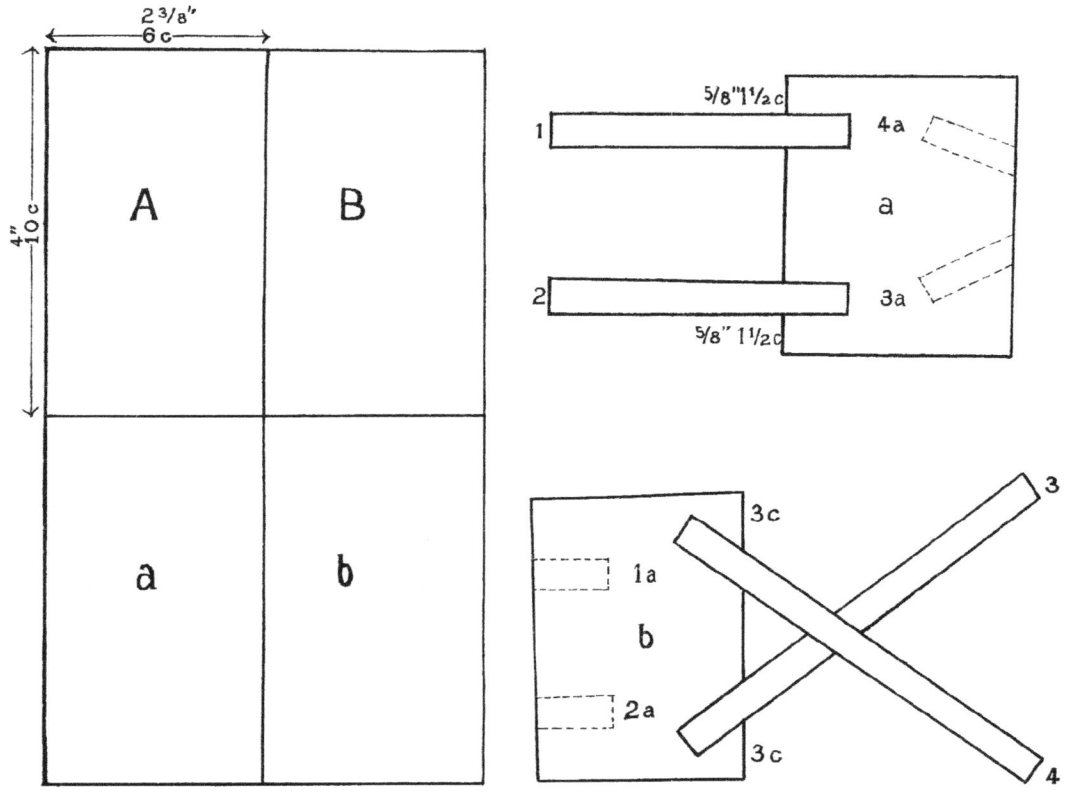

Half size of Model

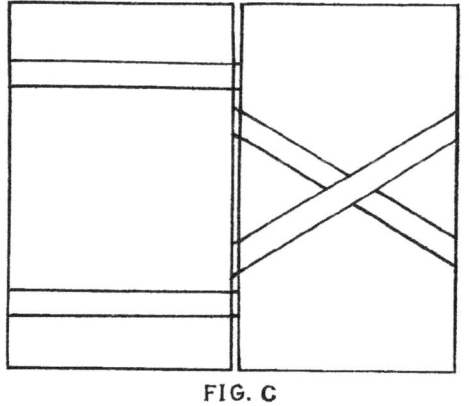

FIG. C

MODEL No. 9

SQUARE TRAY

10 c. x 10 c. x 2 c. (4 in. x 4 in. x ¾ in.)

1. Describe a square *ABCD* of 14 c. (5 ½ in.) on the cardboard.

2. Set off from each angle a distance of 2 c. (3/4 in.) and join.

3. Cut out along the thickened lines, taking care that the cuts are clean and that the corners come away without fraying.

4. Cut gently along *EF*, *FH*, *GH*, *EG*, cutting half or three parts through.

5. Bend the flaps backward from the cuts, and fit corners so as not to overlap but just to meet.

6. Bind the perpendicular corners outside.

7. Bind the top edge with one piece of binding, cutting out triangular pieces so as to join neatly in inner corner. This single strip strengthens the box, and holds the sides together firmly,

8. Bind the lower outside edge so as to cover the lines of half-cuts, and join binding along diagonals.

9. Bind the inside lower edge, the binding fitting equally on the sides and bottom of the tray.

CARDBOARD MODELLING

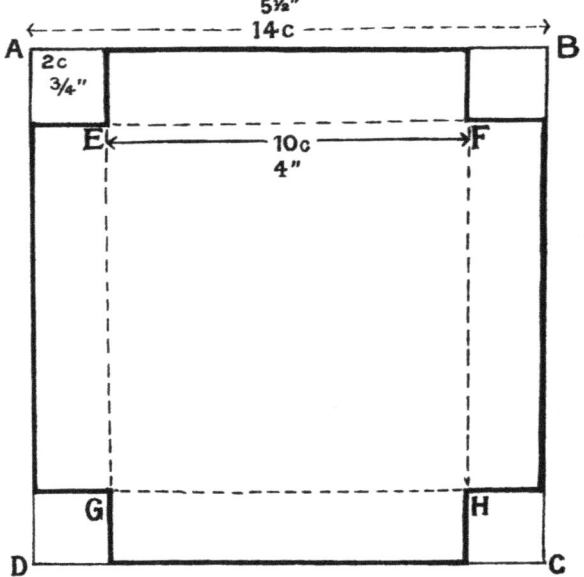

Half size of Model

MODEL No. 10

SQUARE TRAY—with sloping side

$$\left. \begin{array}{l} \text{BASE } 9\text{ c.} \times 9\text{ c.} \\ \text{UPPER EDGE } 13\text{ c.} \times 13\text{ c.} \end{array} \right\} \times 3\text{ c. SIDES}$$

$$\left(\left. \begin{array}{l} 3\tfrac{1}{2}\text{ in.} \times 3\tfrac{1}{2}\text{ in.} \\ 5\ 1/8\text{ in.} \times 5\ 1/8\text{ in.} \end{array} \right\} \times 1\ 3/16\text{ in.} \right)$$

1. Cut out a square of 15 c. (5 7/8 in.)

2. Set off from each angle 3 c. (1 3/16 in.) on each side, and draw lines across dotting the lines of the inner square.

3. From each angle set off 1 c. (3/8 in.) on each side and draw lines to each point thus found from the angles of the inner square.

4. Cut out the corners neatly along the thick lines from *A, B, C, D*.

5. Cut gently along the dotted lines, half or three parts through.

6. Bend the sides backward from these cuts so that corners meet exactly.

7. Bind the outside corners.

8. Bind inside corners.

9. Bind the upper edge with one strip, cutting out so as to fit exactly.

10. Bind inside lower edge with separate strips.

11. Bind outside lower edge with separate strips so as to cover the lines of half-cuts.

CARDBOARD MODELLING

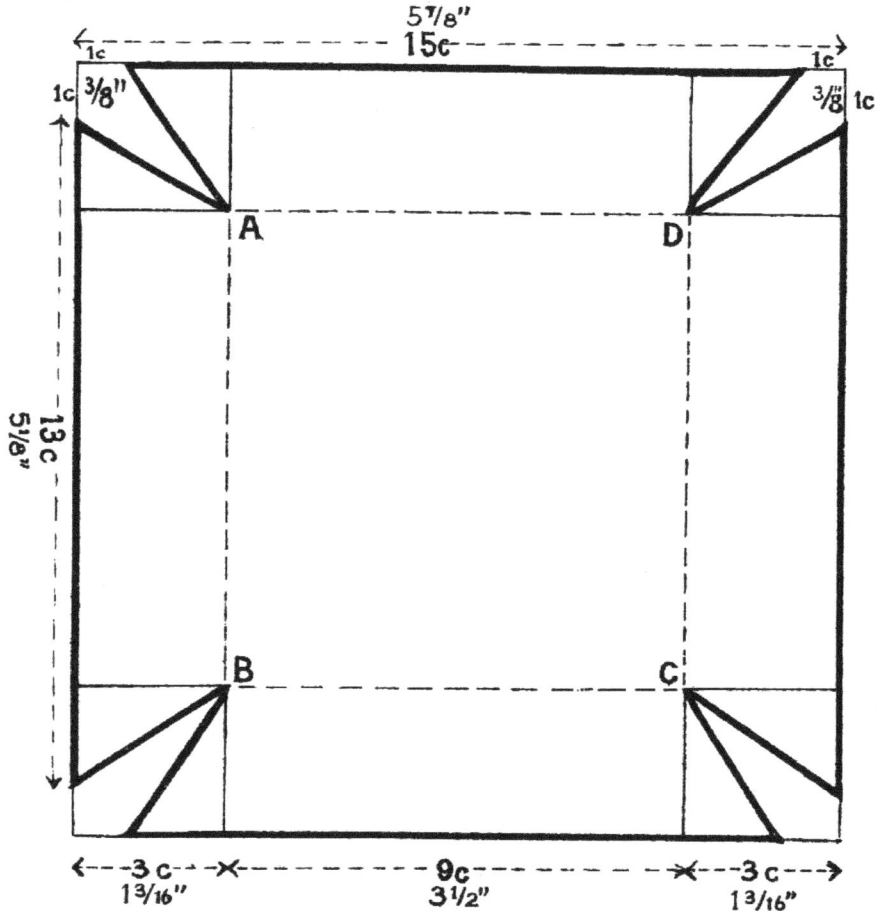

Half size of Model

MODEL No. 11

OBLONG TRAY—with sloping sides

TOP 22 c. x 12 c. (8 ¾ in. x 4 ¾ in.)
BASE 18 c. x 8 c. (7 1/8 in. x 3 1/8 in.)
SIDES 3 c. (1 3/16 in.)

1. Cut out an oblong 24 c. x 14 c. (9 ½ in. x 5 ½ in.)

2. Set off 3 c. (1 3/16 in.) from each angle along each side.

3. Rule lines from these points, so as to mark off the base of the tray 18 c. x 8 c. (7 1/8 in. x 3 1/8 in.) *A, B, C, D.*

4. Set off from each angle 1 c. (3/8 in.) on each side and draw lines to these points from *A, B, C, D.*

5. Cut out the corners neatly along the thickened lines.

6. Cut gently along the dotted lines (describing the bottom of the tray) half or three parts through.

7. Bend the sides and ends backward from the cuts, and fit corners neatly, so as to meet and not overlap.

8. Bind the outside corners.

9. Bind the inside corners.

10. Bind the upper edge with one strip, fitting neatly in inside of each corner.

11. Bind inside lower edge with separate strips fitting exactly along the line of junction.

12. Bind outside lower edge with separate strips so as to cover lines of half-cuts.

CARDBOARD MODELLING

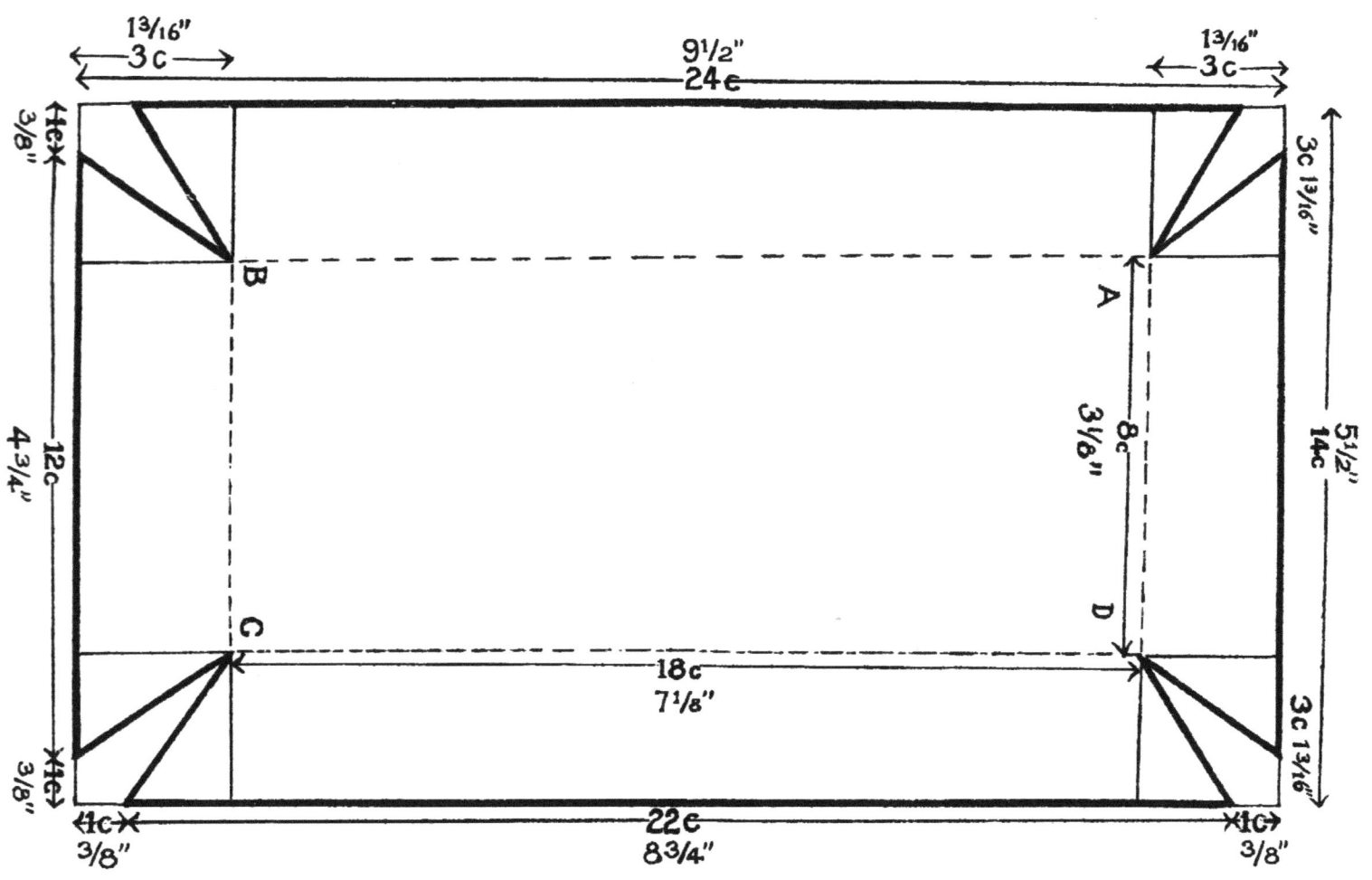

Half size of Model

51

MODEL No. 11a

OBLONG TRAY—with sloping sides

TOP 23 c. x 8 c.
BASE 20 c. x 5 c. } 3 c. SIDES

(TOP 9 in. x 3 1/8 in.
BASE 7 7/8 in. x 2 in. } 1 3/16 in. SIDES)

1. Cut out an oblong 26 c. x. 11 c. (10 ¼ in. x 4 3/8 in.)

2. Set off from each angle 3 c. (1 3/16 in.)

3. Draw lines for inner oblong from these points, giving base of tray, 20 c. x 5 c. (7 7/8 in. x 2 in.), dotted lines.

4. Set off from each angle 1 ½ c. (5/8 in.) along each side, and draw lines to these points from the adjacent angle of inner oblong.

5. Cut out along thickened lines.

6. Cut half or three parts through along dotted lines.

7. Fold backward from the cuts and fit corners so as to meet.

8. Bind as in No. 11.

CARDBOARD MODELLING

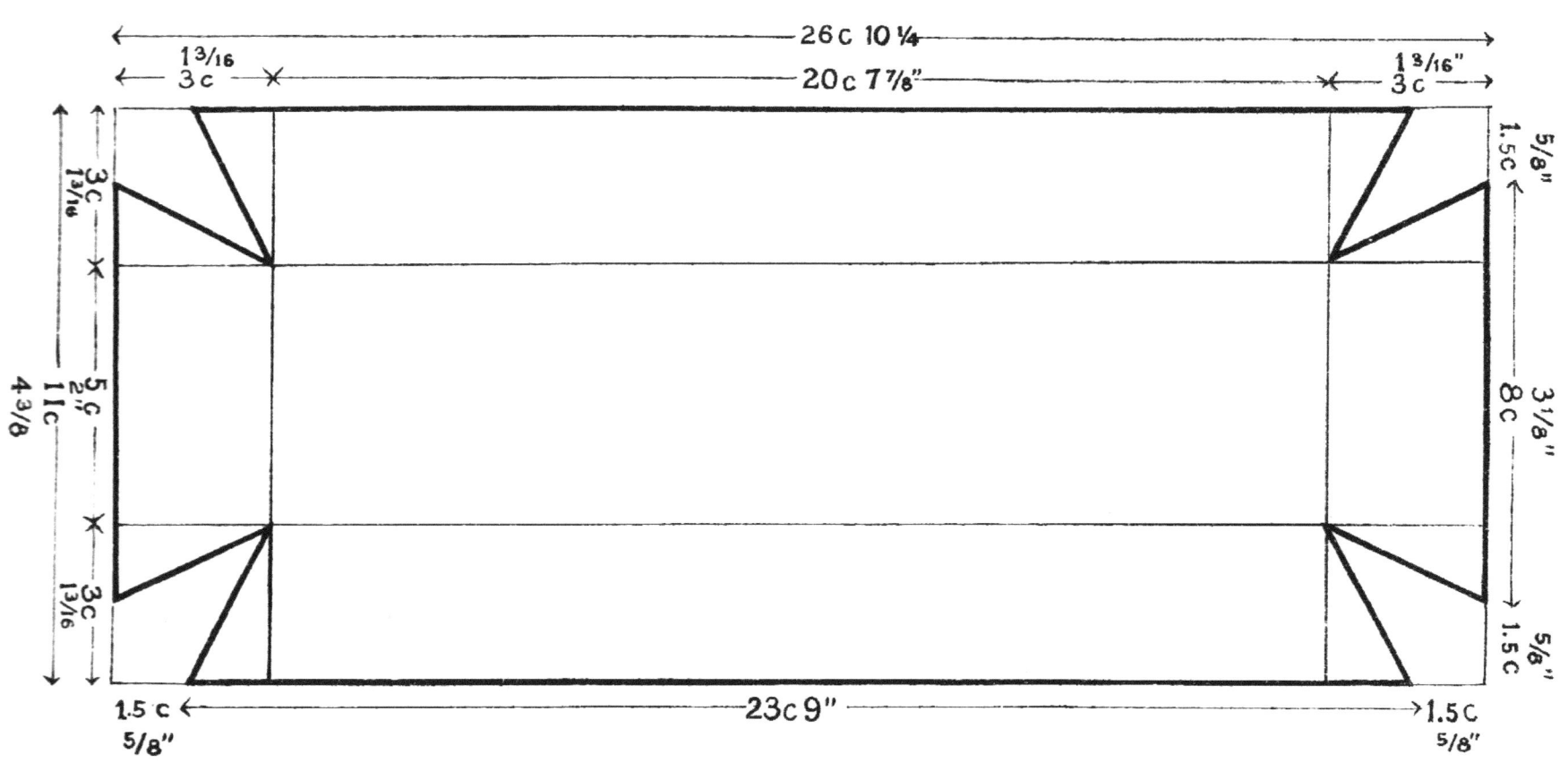

Half size of Model

MODEL No. 12

THREE KEY LABELS

(a) RHOMBUS—5 c. x 5 c. (2 in. x 2 in.)

(b) RHOMBOID—6 c. x 5 c. (2 3/8 in. x 2 in.)

(c) TRAPEZOID—6 c. x 5 c. x 4 c. (2 3/8 in. x 2 in. x 1 5/8 in.)

1. Describe an oblong *ABCD*, 17 c. x 5 c. (6 ¾ in. x 2 in.).
2. Set out, along *AB*, distances of 5 c., 6 c., 6 c. (2 in, 2 3/8 in., 2 3/8 in.)
3. Set out, along *CD*, distances of 1 c. from each end (3/8 in.)
4. From the point 1 c. from *C*, set off distances of 5 c., 6 c., 4 c (2 in., 2 3/8 in., 2 5/8 in.)
5. Join these points across the oblong.
6. Cut out along the thick lines.
7. Bind the edges of each figure cut out.
8. A small hole should be punched in one of the angles.

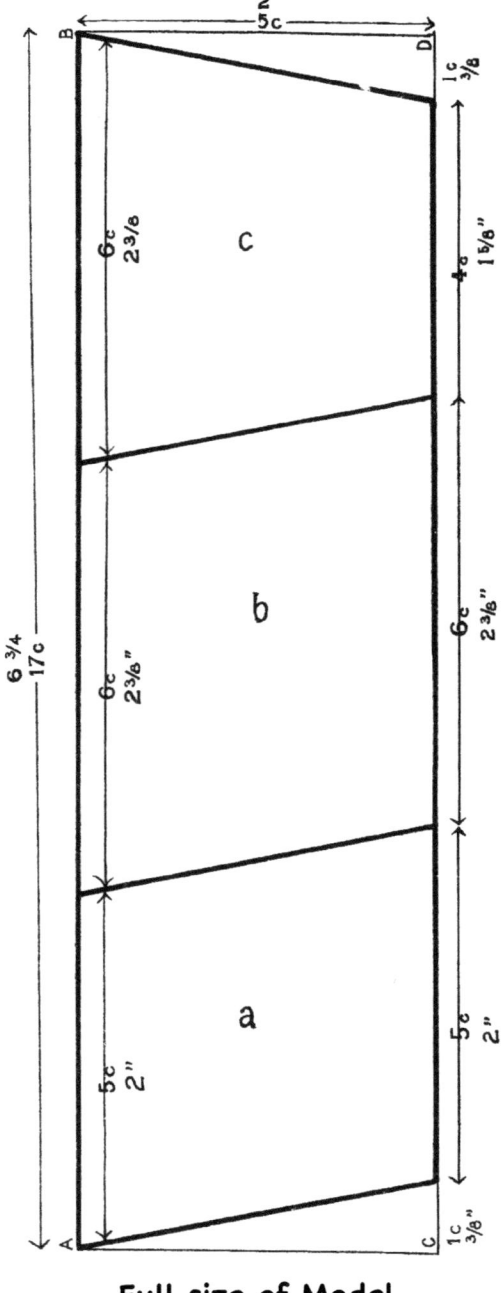

Full size of Model

MODEL No. 13

PORTFOLIO

23 c. x 18 c. (9 in. x 7 1/8 in.)

1. Cut out two oblongs *B*, *C*, 23 c. x 18 c. (9 in. x 7 1/8 in.)

2. From an oblong 23 c. x 5 c. (9 in. x 2 in.) cut out the flap *A* by setting off from each corner 3.5 c. (1 3/8 in.) along longer side, and 2 c. (3/4 in.) along shorter side, and cutting along the lines joining these points across each corner.

3. Bind shorter sides of the two oblongs and one long side *kl* of oblong *C*.

4. Bind flap *A*, except along *ab*.

5. Cut two cloth strips 25 c. x 5 c. (9 7/8 in. x 2 in.)

6. Join the three parts *A, B, C,* with these cloth strips, leaving spaces *m, n*, of 3 c. (1 1/8 in.) and overlapping 1 c. at each end.

7. Cut two strips of enamel paper 22 c. x 5 c. (8 5/8 in. x 2 in.) and fix over spaces *m* and *n* so as to cover in unbound edges and meet binding at each end.

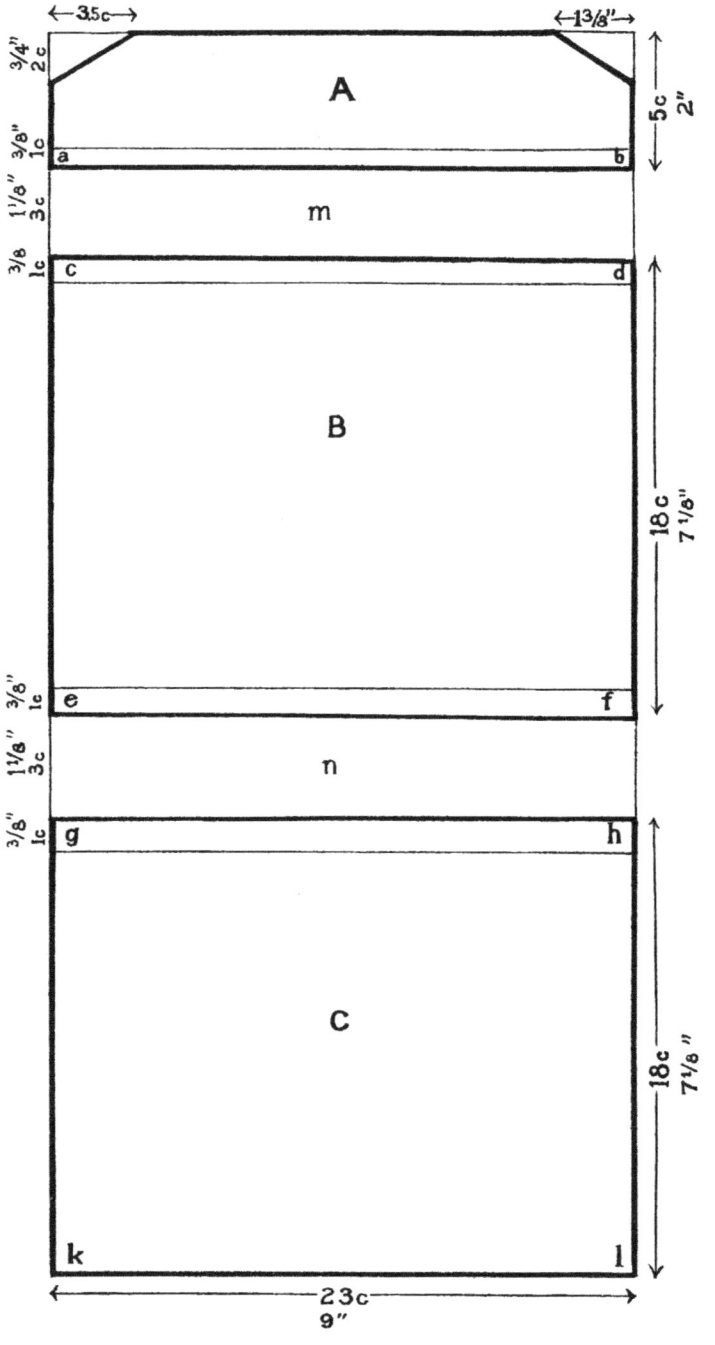

One third size of Model

MODEL No. 14

HEXAGONAL LAMP MAT

8 c. RADIUS (3 1/8 in.)

1. Describe a circle with a radius of 8 c. (3 1/8 in.)

2. From any point in the circumference set off distances equal to the radius.

3. Join these points in consecutive order.

4. Bind.

5. Fit the binding along the lines joining opposite angles.

The inner hexagon is inserted to show binding and manner of joining.

CARDBOARD MODELLING

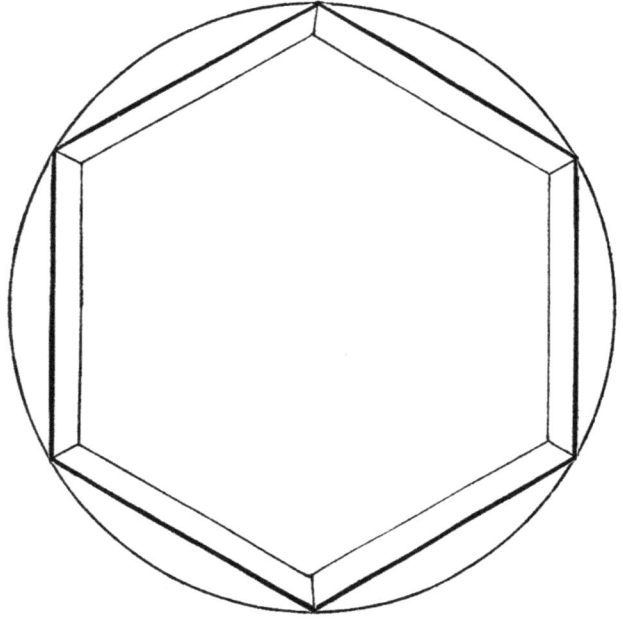

Half size of Model

MODEL No. 14a

HEXAGONAL TRAY—with Perpendicular Sides

9 c. RADIUS, UPPER EDGE (3 ½ in.)

6 c. RADIUS, BASE (2 3/8 in.)

3 c. SIDES (1 1/8 in.)

1. Describe two concentric circles—inner circle with a radius of 6 c. (2 3/8 in.), outer 9 c. (3 ½ in.).

2. Inscribe hexagon in inner circle with 6 c. sides, and within outer circle a circumscribing hexagon of 9 c., by producing lines through opposite angles of inner hexagon.

3. Set off 1 ½ c. from each angle of the outer hexagon, by drawing lines through each angle of the inner hexagon and the next alternate angle.

4. Cut out along thickened lines, neatly and with clean angles.

5. Cut half or three parts through along the dotted lines of the inner hexagon.

6. Bend backward from the cuts, and fit neatly at the angles.

7. Bind outside angles.

8. Bind inside angles.

9. Bind upper edge with separate strips exactly meeting at lines of juncture.

10. Bind inside lower edge with separate strips fitting neatly at the angles.

11. Bind outside lower edge with separate strips fitting evenly along lines of juncture, and on lines from each angle to opposite angle along the base.

CARDBOARD MODELLING

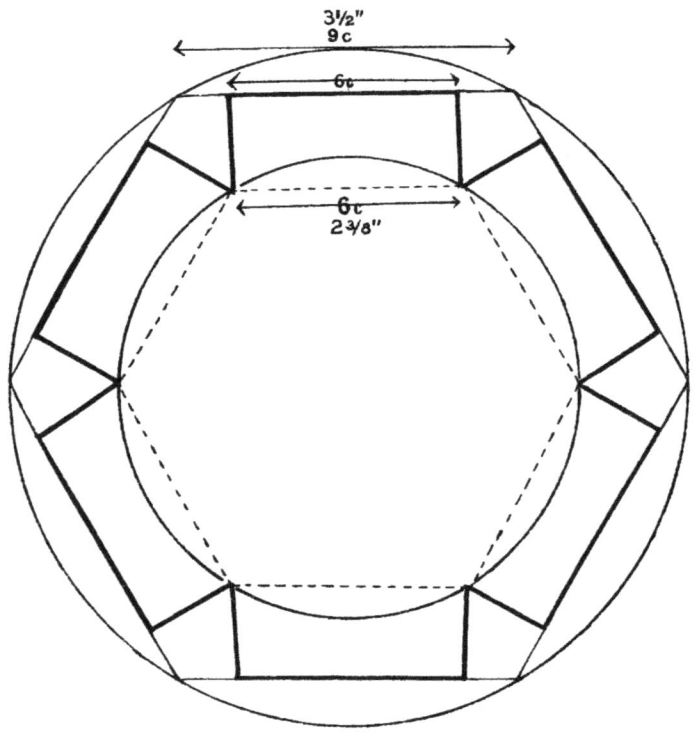

Half size of Model

MODEL No. 15

HEXAGONAL TRAY—with sloping sides
10 c. x 6 c. RADII (3 7/8 in. x 2 3/8 in.)
UPPER EDGE 8 c. (3 1/8 in.)
LOWER EDGE 6 c. (2 3/8 in.)

1. Describe concentric circles having 6 c. (2 3/8 in.) and 10 c. (3 7/8 in.) radii respectively.

2. Set off their respective hexagons within each circle, beginning with the inner hexagon and transferring across the angles to the outer circle for the outer hexagon.

3. Set off 1 c. (3/8 in.) from each angle along each side of the outer hexagon.

4. Join each of these points with the nearest angle of the inner hexagon.

5. Dot the lines of the inner hexagon for the base of the tray.

6. Thicken the cutting lines of the outer hexagon from the point 1 c. distant from each angle, and the lines joining these points with the angles of the inner hexagon.

7. Cut out the figure shown in thickened lines.

8. Cut half or three parts through along the dotted lines.

9. Bend sides backward from the half-cuts, and fit neatly at the angles.

10. Bind outer sloping angles.

11. Bind inner angles.

12. Bind upper edge with separate strips exactly meeting at line of junction.

13. Bind inside lower edge with separate strips fitting neatly at the angles.

14. Bind outside lower edge with separate strips fitting exactly at lines of junction on lines from each angle to opposite angle along the base.

CARDBOARD MODELLING

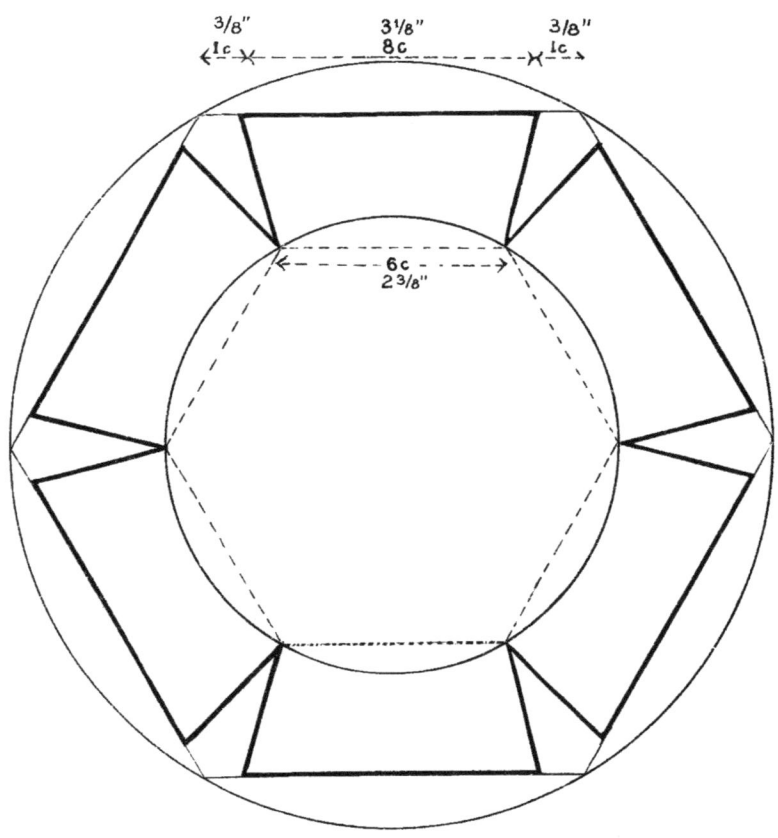

Half size of Model

MODEL No. 16

OCTAGONAL LAMP MAT

8 c. RADIUS (3 1/8 in.)   6 c. SIDES (2 3/8 in.)

1. With a radius of 8 c. (3 1/8 in.) describe a circle.

2. Draw diameters at right angles, and bisect two of the angles formed at the center of the circle.

3. Draw lines through the center and points of bisection, cutting the circle on opposite sides.

4. Complete the octagon by drawing lines joining the consecutive points thus obtained on the circle.

5. Cut out the octagon.

6. Bind the edges as in Model No. 14, so that the joins of the binding are along the lines joining opposite angles.

CARDBOARD MODELLING

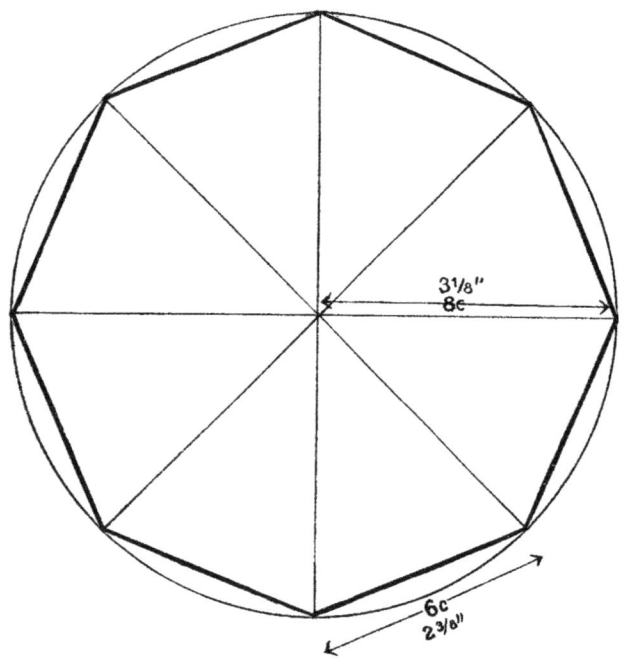

MODEL No. 17

MATCH POCKET

14 c. x 9 c. (5 ½ in. x 3 ½ in.)

1. Describe an oblong (Fig. 1) 14 c. x 9 c. (5 ½ in. x 3 ½ in.)

2. Set off from each angle a distance of 1 ½ c. (9/16 in.) along each side, and join across the angle.

3. Cut out along the thickened lines. (This is the back of the pocket, the inner thin line shows appearance when bound.)

4. Bind the edges.

5. At a distance of 3.5 c. (1 3/8 in.) from one end, and 6 ½ c. (2 ½ in.) from the other, draw parallels to show position of pocket.

6. For the pocket, describe an oblong (Fig. 2) 10 c (3 7/8 in.) long, and of a width equal to the distance across the back of the pocket from binding to binding about 8.2 c. (3 ¼ in.)

7. In this oblong set off from the top one distance of 4 c. (1 5/8 in.), and three each 2 c. (3/4 in.), and draw lines across forming strips C,D,E,F. (C is the back of the pocket to be affixed to position defined in (5); D, E, and F form the front and bottom of the pocket.)

8. Along each end of C set off distances from the top of 0.75 c., 2 c., 1.25 c., (3/8 in., ¾ in., ½ in.), and from these points draw lines perpendicular to the ends of the strip C of 4.2 c., 3.5 c., and 2 c. (1 5/8 in., 1 3/8 in., ¾ in.).

9. Cut out the whole figure along the thickened lines, and half or three parts through along dotted lines.

10. Bend the sides *A* and *B* back from the half-cuts.

11. Bend *D, E, F* back from the half-cuts so that the angles *A* and *B* meet corresponding angles in *A* and *B*. *z to z', y to y', x to x', etc.*

12. Bind outside the lines of half-cuts.

13. Bind firmly over the ends of these bindings and along the junctions of the sides with the front and bottom of the pocket.

14. With one strip bind the upper edge of the pocket so as to strengthen the whole.

15. Glue the back *C* firmly to position on back (No. 5).

16. Glue an oblong of fine sandpaper to the back, below the pocket at *a, b, c, d*.

17. Punch a small hole at *e*.

CARDBOARD MODELLING

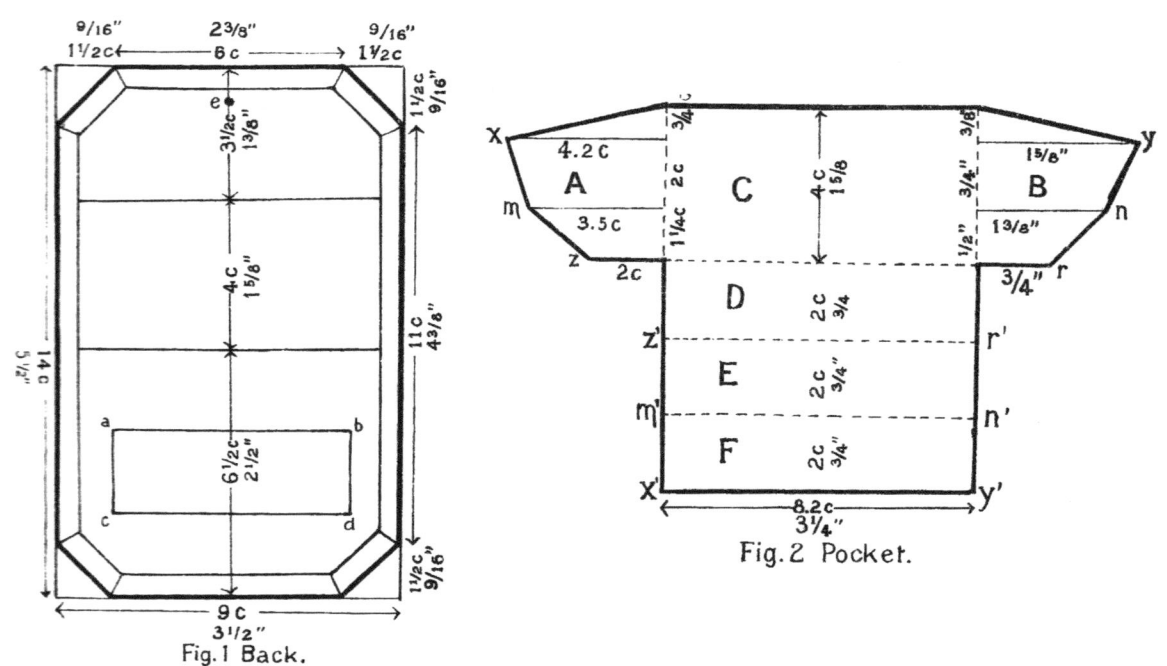

Fig. 1 Back.

Fig. 2 Pocket.

Half size of Model

MODEL No. 18
BOX WITH LID

BOX 9 c. x 6 x. x 3 c. (3 ½ in. x 2 3/8 in. x 1 3/16 in.)

LID 9 ½ c. x 6 ½ c. x 1 ½ c. (3 ¾ in. x 2 ½ in. x 5/8 in.)

1. Describe and cut out an oblong 15 c. (5 7/8 in.) x 12 c. (4 ¾ in.)
2. Set off 3 c. (1 3/16 in.) from each angle along each side.
3. Draw lines across from these points so as to form an inner oblong—the bottom of the box—of 9 c. x 6 c. (Fig. 1).
4. Cut out the squares *A, B, C, D* neatly.
5. Cut half or three parts through along the dotted lines.
6. Bend sides backwards from the cuts and fit at the angles.
7. Bind outside perpendicular corners.
8. Bind the upper edge with one strip fitting neatly within the angles.
9. Bind outside lower edge to cover lines of half-cuts.
10. Describe and cut out an oblong of 12.5 c. x 9.5 c. (4 7/8 in. x 3 ¾ in.)
11. Set off 1 ½ c. (9/16 in.) from each angle along each side.
12. Draw lines across as in Fig. 2.
13. Cut out the corner squares neatly.
14. Cut half or three parts through along dotted lines, for the top of the lid.
15. Proceed as in Directions 1, 7, 8 and 9.

CARDBOARD MODELLING

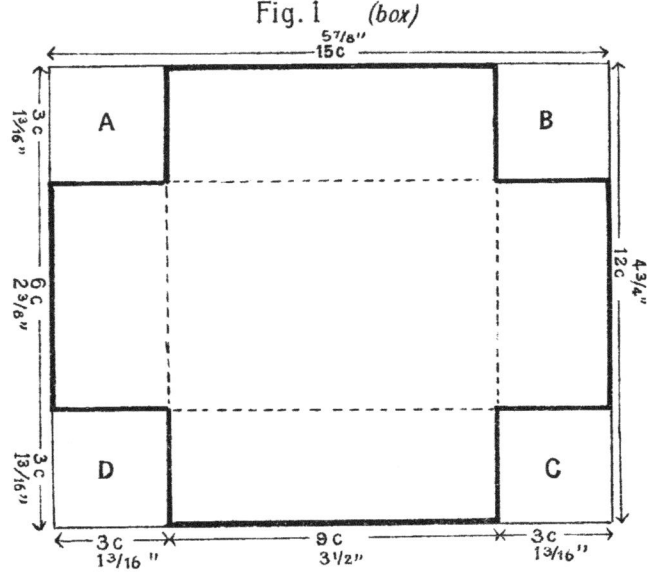

Fig. 1 (box)

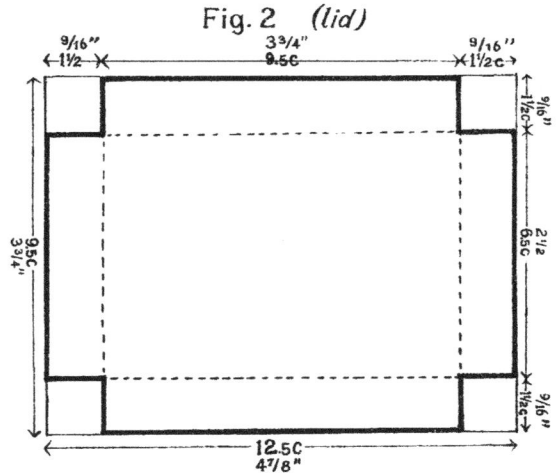

Fig. 2 (lid)

Half size of Model

MODEL No. 19

OBLONG BOX--with hinge lid and falling front

10 c. x 7 c. x 3.5 c. (4 in. x 2 ¾ in. x 1 3/8 in.)

1. Describe an oblong 17 c. x 14 c. (6 ¾ in. x 5 ½ in.)

2. Set off from each angle along each side distances of 3.5 c. (1 3/8 in.)

3. Join these points across the oblong by lines parallel to the sides, forming an inner oblong of 10 c. (4 in.) x 7 c. (2 ¾ in.) for the bottom of the box.

4. Cut out along the thick lines and half or three parts through along the dotted lines. Strip *A* must be cut clean away to form the hinged front.

5. Bend sides *B, C, D* backward from the cuts and bind outside corners.

6. Bind upper edge and along the edges forming open front of box.

7. Bind outside lower edge.

8. Bind strip *A* all round, and join to the outside of the bottom of the box by a strip of cloth 2 c. (3/4 in.) wide.

9. For the lid describe an oblong 13.5 c. x 9 c. (5 3/8 in. x 3 ½ in.).

10. From each angle set off at *a* and *b* along each side and at *c* and *d* alongside cd only, distances of 1.5 c. (5/8 in.). From the points found in *ab* draw lines to *cd* parallel to the sides, forming an inner oblong of 10.5 c. x 7.5 c.

11. From *c* and *d* set off along the sides of the oblong distances 1.5 c. (5/8 in.), and join to the ends of the dotted lines.

12. Cut out along the thick lines, and half or three parts through along the dotted lines. Cut out across the angles at *c* and *d*.

13. Bend back the sides from the half-cuts, and bind outside angles.

14. Bind outside cut edge, and outer edge along half-cuts.

15. Fix the lid at *cd* to the upper edge of the box at *c'd'* by means of a 2 c. (3/4 in.) strip of cloth, so that the edges of lid and box are a very little apart and lid works freely.

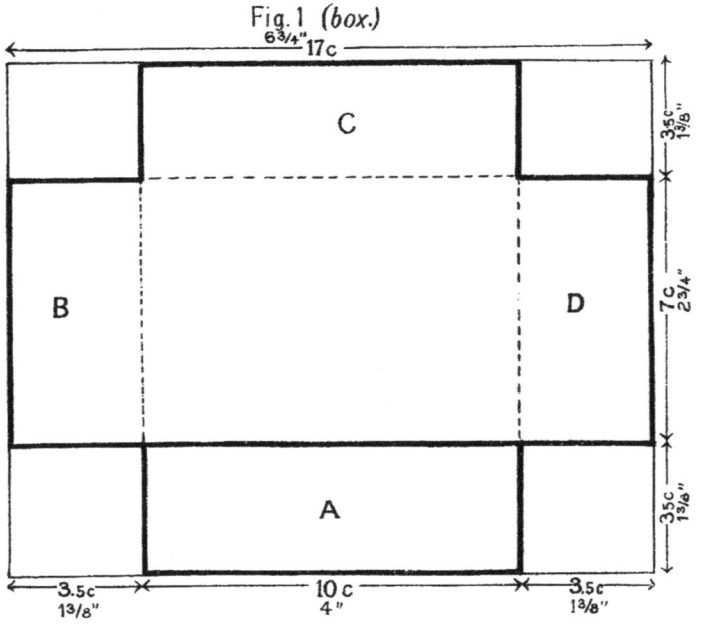
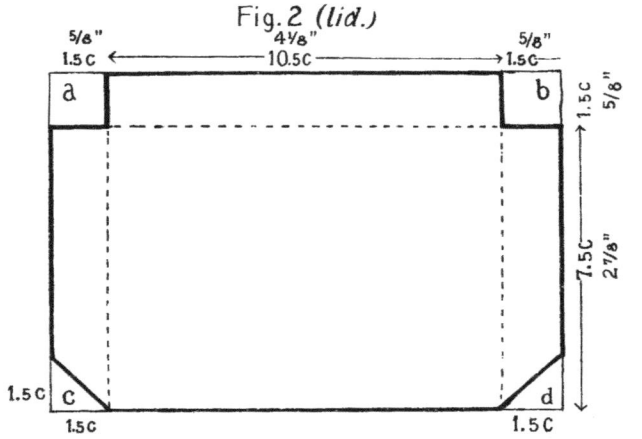

Half size of Model

MODEL No. 20

NEEDLE CASE

8 c. x 5 c. (3 1/8 in. x 2 in.)

1. Cut out two oblongs, each 8 c. x 5 c. (3 1/8 in. x 2 in.)

2. Join these by a 3 c. (1 1/8 in.) strip of cloth overlapping 1 c. within at each end, and leaving 1 c. between the two oblongs.

3. Cover the inside of this join with a 3 c. (1 1/8 in.) strip of cloth.

4. Cover the outsides with black cloth, folding over 1 c. (3/8 in.) on each side and on the long side away from the hinge strip.

5. Cover each inside with red morocco paper or thin cloth, within a very short distance of each edge.

6. Add a silk or elastic band and a piece of thin flannel.

CARDBOARD MODELLING

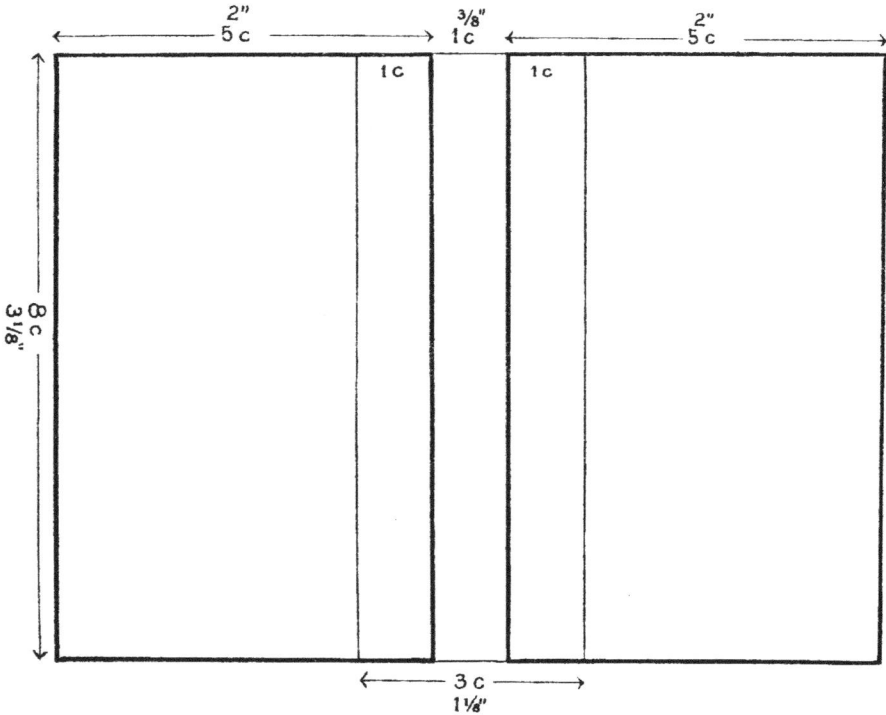

Full size of Model

MODEL No. 21

POCKET MIRROR

9 c. x 5.5 c. (3 ½ in. x 2 1/8 in.)

1. Cut out two oblong pieces of cardboard each 9 c. x 5.5 c. (3 ½ in. x 2 1/8 in.)

2. Through *ab* 2.5 c. (1 in.) from the end of one of these oblongs cut through the board.

3. Bind the small piece thus cut off on all sides, except *a, b*.

4. Bind the remaining pieces on each long side.

5. Join the small bound piece *A* to the remaining piece of the oblong *B*, by a 1.5 c. (5/8 in.) strip of cloth, so that the two touch when closed and the ends of the strip overlap within.

6. For *D* cut a strip of board 5.5 c. x 1 c. (2 1/8 in. x 3/8 in.) and bind the ends.

7. Glue this in position *D* and cover with cloth 5.5 c. long and coming 0.5 c. further on the inner face of *C* and 1.5 c. on the outer face = 3 c. (1 1/8 in.) wide.

8. Join *C* and *B* by a strip of cloth 3 c. (1 1/8 in.) wide overlapping 1 c. (3/8 in.) on the inside at each end, and leaving 1 c. (3/8 in.) between the two oblongs. Cover inside of this join by cloth strip.

9. Take a small mirror 7 c. x 5.5 c. (2 ¾ in. x 2 1/8 in.), cover the back with black cloth, or paper, and bind the edges.

10. Glue this mirror to *ef* so that the mirror lies over *B*.

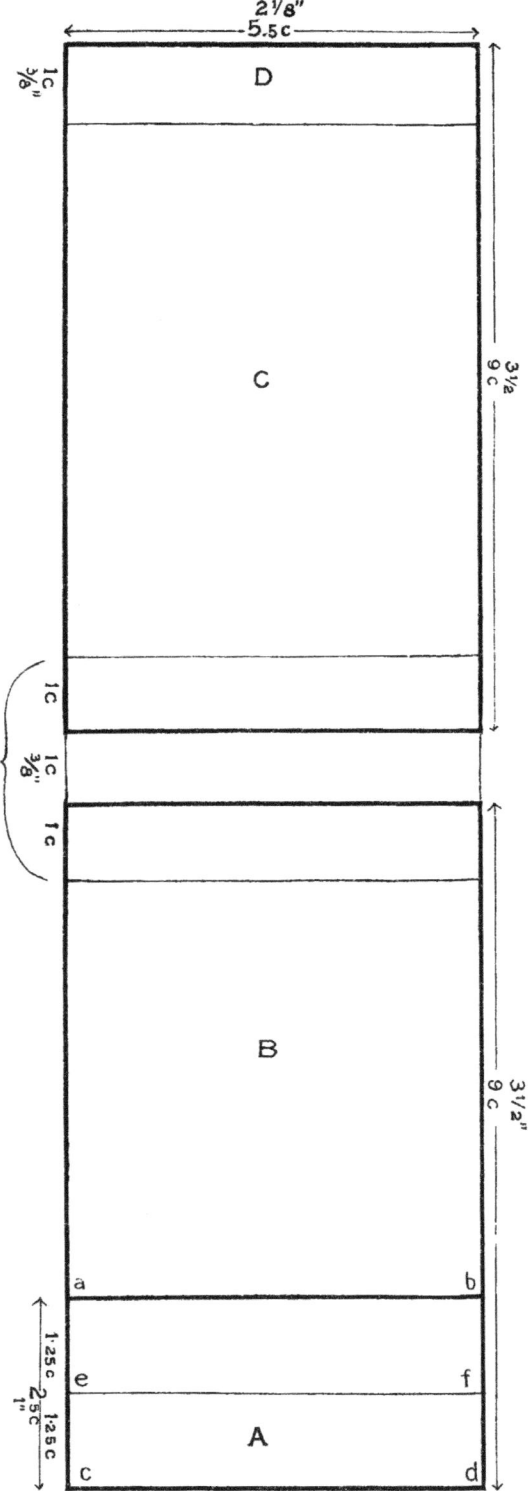

Full size of Model

75

MODEL No. 22

STATIONERY PORTFOLIO—with pocket

23 c. x 18 c. (9 in. x 7 1/8 in.)

1. Cut out, as in Model No. 13, two oblongs each 18 c. x 23 c. (7 1/8 in. x 9 in.) and one oblong 23 c. x 5 c. (9 in. x 2 in.) for flap *A*.

2. Bind one 23 c. side *ab* of one of the larger oblongs *C*.

3. From each of two corners on one long side of *A* set off 2 c. (3/4 in.) along each side. Join across the angles, and cut out.

4. Bind *A*, except along the 23 c. side *kl*.

5. Cut one strip of binding 25 c. x 5 c. (9 7/8 in. x 2 in.).

6. Join *A* to *B* by this strip, keeping *A* and *B* 3 c. (1 1/8 in.) apart, and binding overlapping 1 c. (3/8 in.) at each end, and 1 c. (3/8 in.) from the sides *kl*, *gh*.

7. Cut a strip of enamel paper 22.5 c. x 5 c. (8 7/8 in. x 2 in.) to cover these joins.

8. Cut a strip of binding 61 c. x 5 c. (24 ½ in. x 2 in.).

9. Join *ef* and *cd* in the center of this strip, leaving 3 c. of binding between the two, and allowing binding to cover 1 c. along each board.

10. When quite dry fold this joining along the middle longitudinally and so as to fall within the boards *B* and *C*.

11. Bring the side *ab* over to *gk* and bind 1 c. (3/8 in.) along the short sides of each board, the ends of the binding to be folded over and fixed firmly within the pocket.

CARDBOARD MODELLING

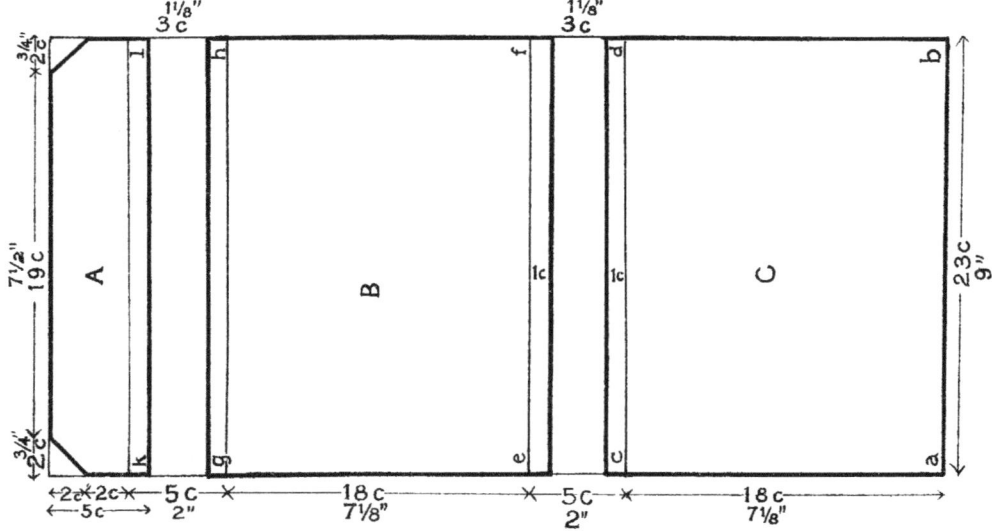

One quarter size of Model

MODEL No. 23

PEN AND INK TRAY

21 c. x 11 c. { 4 c. BACK / 2 c. FRONT   (8 ¼ in. x 4 3/8 in. { 1 5/8 in. / 3/4 in.)

1. Cut out an oblong 29 c. x 17 c. (11 ½ in. x 6 ¾ in.).
2. At each end of *A* set off 4 c. (1 5/8 in.) along each side, and draw lines parallel to sides, forming strips *A, E, F*.
3. Set off distance of 5 c. (2 in.) from strip *A* along *E* and *F*.
4. At the other angles of the oblong set off 2 c. (3/4 in.) distances along each short side, and join to form strip *D*.
5. In *E* and *F* set off 2 c. (3/4 in.) distances along this line, and join points thus formed with the 5 c. points found in Direction 3.
6. Cut out along thickened lines, and half or three parts through along dotted lines.
7. Cut out a separate strip of cardboard 21 c. x 4 c. (8 ¼ in. x 1 5/8 in.) and bind one long side.
8. Cut out two separate pieces of board 5 c. x 4 c. (2 in. x 1 5/8 in.) and bind one 5 c. edge of each.
9. Set out line *ab* for position of strip in No. 7. And *cd* and *ef* 5 c. (2 in.) from *a* and *b* for strips in No. 8.
10. Bend backwards from half-cuts and fit neatly at the angles.
11. Bind outside corners, outside upper edge, inside lower edge.
12. Fit in strip along *ab*, and fasten with glue.
13. Fit in strips (Direction 8) along *cd* and *ef*, and fasten with glue.
14. Cut out two strips of board 20 c. x 4 c. (7 7/8 in. x 1 5/8 in.), and at three distances of a shade less than 5 c. (2 in.) cut half or three parts through, and bend backwards so as to form box; join the two loose ends and bind round top edge.
15. Fit these boxes into the 5 c. squares formed in *B*, and fasten with a touch of glue.

CARDBOARD MODELLING

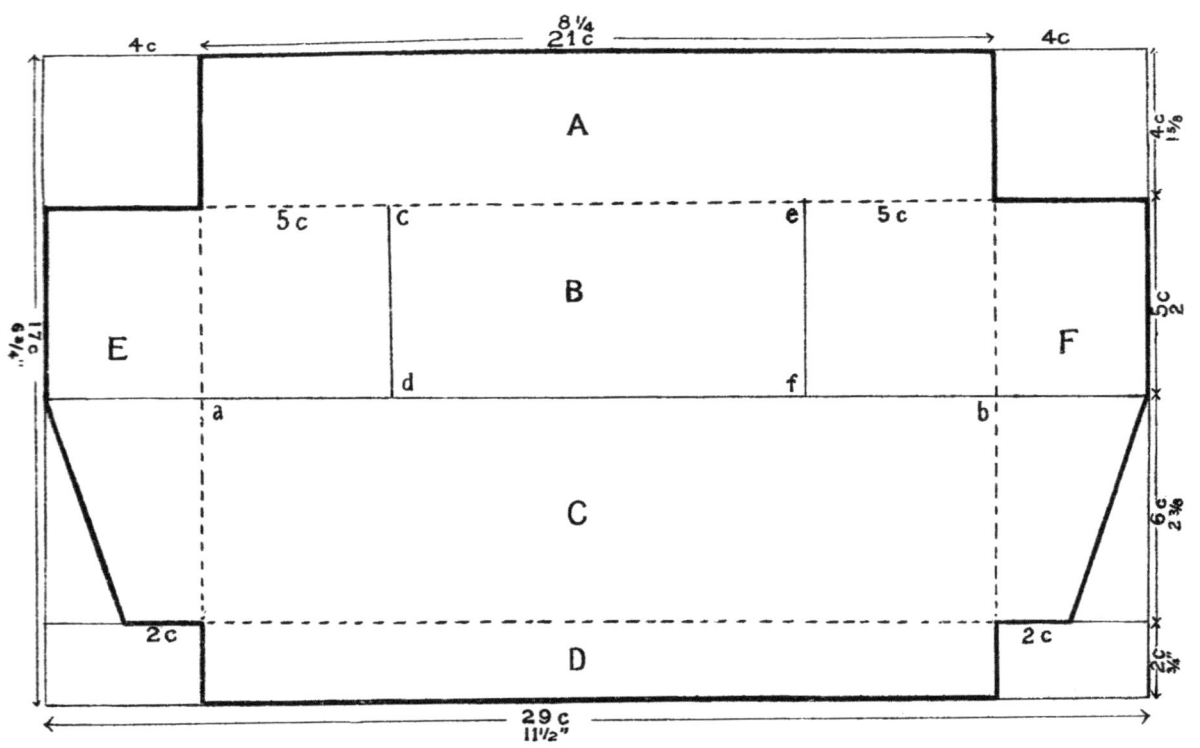

Half size of Model

MODEL No. 24

OBLONG PHOTO FRAME

20.5 c. x 16.5 c. (8 1/8 in. x 6 ½ in.)

1. Cut out an oblong 20.5 c. x 16.5 c. (8 1/8 in. x 6 ½ in.)

2. From each corner set off along each side a distance of 4 c. (1 5/8 in.)

3. Draw lines from these points parallel to sides and forming inner oblong of 12.5 c. x 8.5 c. (4 7/8 in. x 3 ¼ in.)

4. Cut out this inner oblong with great care.

5. Bind edges of these oblongs.

6. Cut out another oblong 16 c. x 10 c. (6 ½ in. x 3 7/8 in.), cover one side with colored paper and bind edges.

7. Cut out another oblong 16 c. x 12 c. (6 ¼ in. x 4 ¾ in.), and bind edges.

8. Cut two strips of cardboard 16 c. x 1 c. (6 ¼ in. x 3/8 in.).

9. Bind these strips along one side, and at the ends.

10. Glue these strips to the back of the model parallel to, and at a distance of half a centimeter (3/16 in.) from, the long sides of the open oblong.

11. Glue the bound board (Direction No. 7) firmly to the top of these strips, and allow glue to set.

12. Insert the board (Direction No. 6) along the slide obtained in Directions 10 and 11, with colored side to the front.

13. Take a strip of binding 7 c. (2 ¾ in.) long, and fold into a loop thus; place the gummed side uppermost, and about the middle bring one part forward and fold at right angles; then bring the same part backward so that the gummed part faces the front, leaving an opening between the two sides; then fasten in the center of one of the long sides.

This model may be varied by cutting short pieces of cardboard (Direction No. 8) 12 c x 1 c. (4 ¾ in. x 3/8 in.) and fastening them ½ c. from the shorter sides of the open oblong. The loop would then be fastened on one of the short sides, so that the slide for the back may be passed into its place with the long sides perpendicular.

CARDBOARD MODELLING

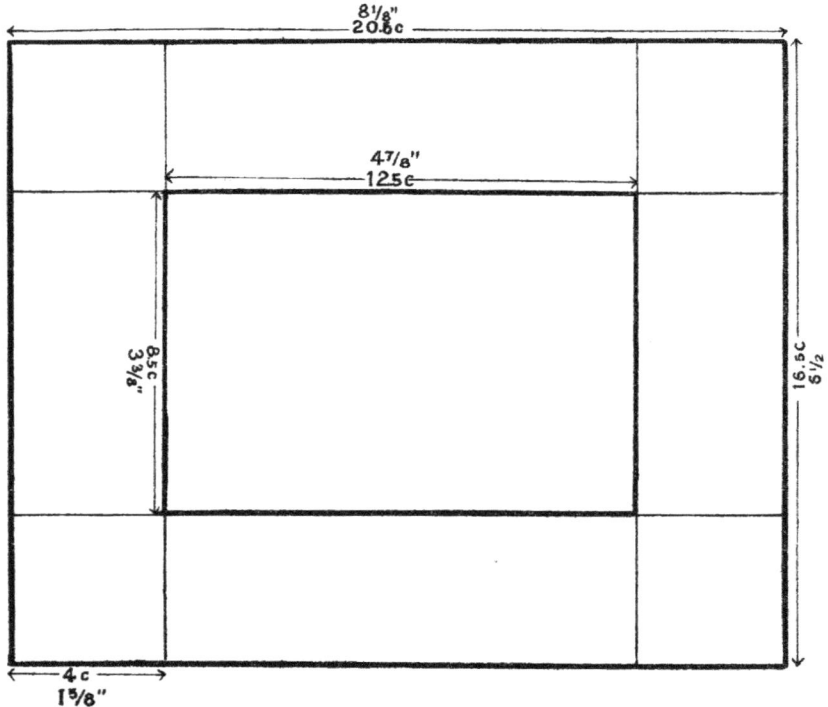

Half size of Model

MODEL No. 25

SHAPED PHOTO FRAME

16 c. x 13 c. (6 ¼ in. x 5 1/8 in.)

1. Describe an oblong 16 c. x 13 c. (6 ¼ in. x 5 1/8 in.)

2. From each angle set off along each side distances of 3.5 c. (1 3/8 in.) and join across the oblong, forming an inner oblong of 9 c. x 6 c. (3 ½ in. x 2 3/8 in.)

3. Set off 1 c. (3/8 in.) from each outer angle along each side of the outer oblong, and join these points to the opposite points by lines drawn parallel to the sides.

4. Cut out along the thick lines, and cut out neatly the inner oblong.

5. Bind all cut edges.

6. Cut out for strips of board, each 13 c. x 1 c. (6 ¼ in. x 3/8 in.) and two each 9 c. x 1 c. (3 ½ in. x 3/8 in.). Glue the two short trips together, and bind the ends and one long side. Glue the long strips together two and two so as to make two long thicker strips, and bind ends and one long side of each.

7. Cut out an oblong of cardboard 13 c. x 10 c. (5 1/8 in. x 4 in.) and bind the edges.

8. Along the two long sides and one short side of this oblong, glue the strips obtained in Direction No. 6, with the binding of the strips along the binding of the back.

9. Cut out a rest for the back 10 c. (4 in.) long, 3 c. (1 1/8 in.) wide at one end, and 5 c. (2 in.) at the other.

10. Bind all the sides of this but the short end.

11. Join this rest to the back by a 3 c. (1 1/8 in.) wide strip of cloth fixed firmly over the narrow end and passing through a slit in the back 3 c. from the top of the back and fastened securely on the lower side of the slit at the back.

12. At 3.5 c. and 2.5 c. from the foot of the rest, cut 1 c. slits, and one 3.5 c. from the bottom of the back. Through these slits pass and fix a 1 c. strip of cloth, and fasten securely on the inside.

13. Glue the whole on the strip side to the back of the frame so as to touch the binding of the latter all round.

14. Cut out an oblong of cardboard 12.5 c. x 8 c. (5 in. x 3 1/8 in.) and bind.

15. Cover one face with red morocco paper or fine red cloth within a very narrow distance of the edge. This forms a slide for the back.

CARDBOARD MODELLING

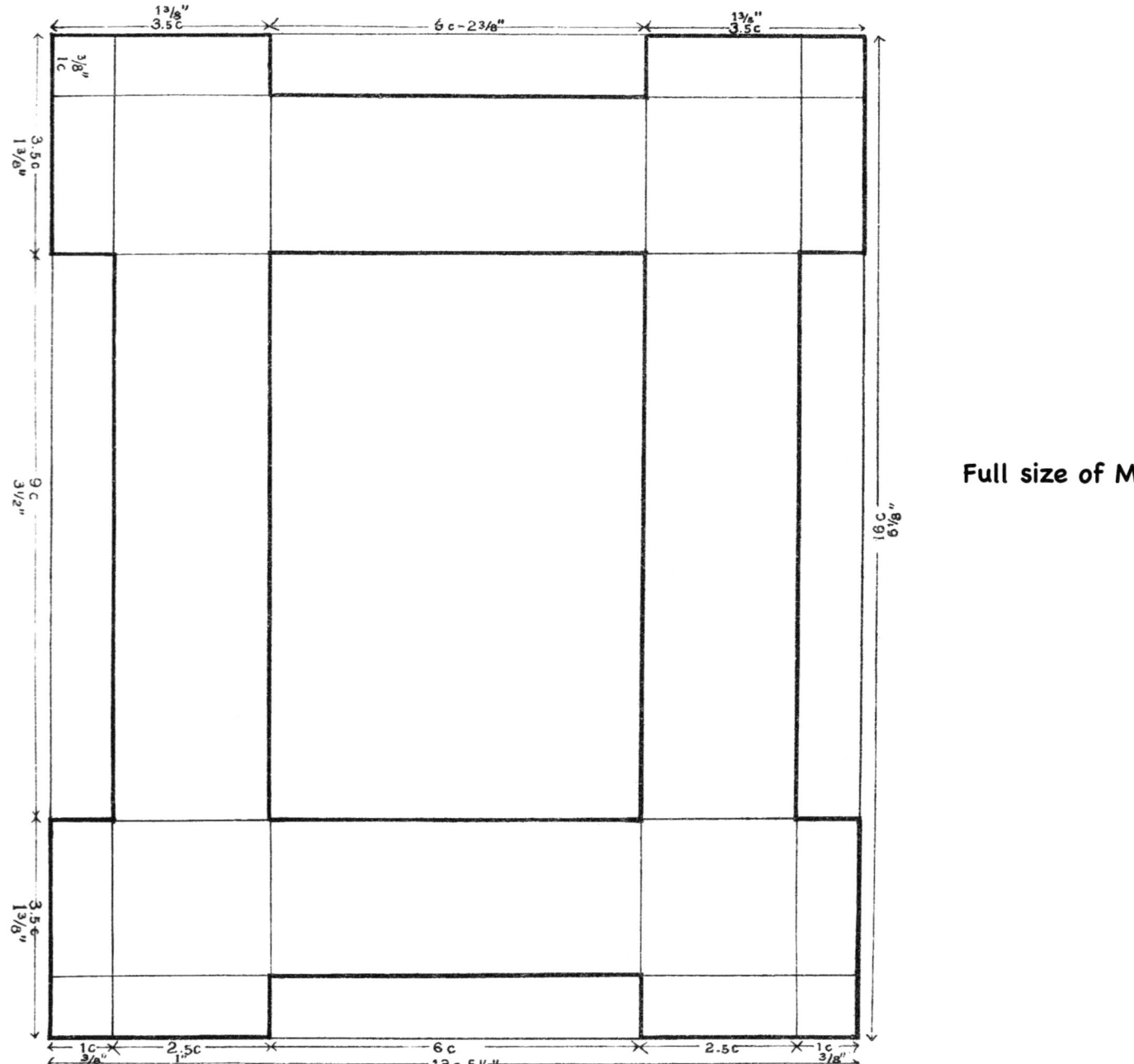

Full size of Model

MODEL No. 26

TRIANGULAR PAPER WEIGHT

11 c. x 11 c. x 15 ½ c. (4 3/8 in. x 4 3/8 in. x 6 1/8 in.)

1. Cut out four right-angled triangles, the sides containing the right angle in each to be 11 c. (4 3/8 in.).

2. Glue these four triangles firmly and evenly together.

3. Cut a strip of binding 38 c. x 3 c. (15 in. x 1 1/8 in.)

4. Bind in one piece, beginning at the right angle, and cutting out to fit along lines from angles to inner edge of binding, which should cover 1.25 c. from the edges of each face.

CARDBOARD MODELLING

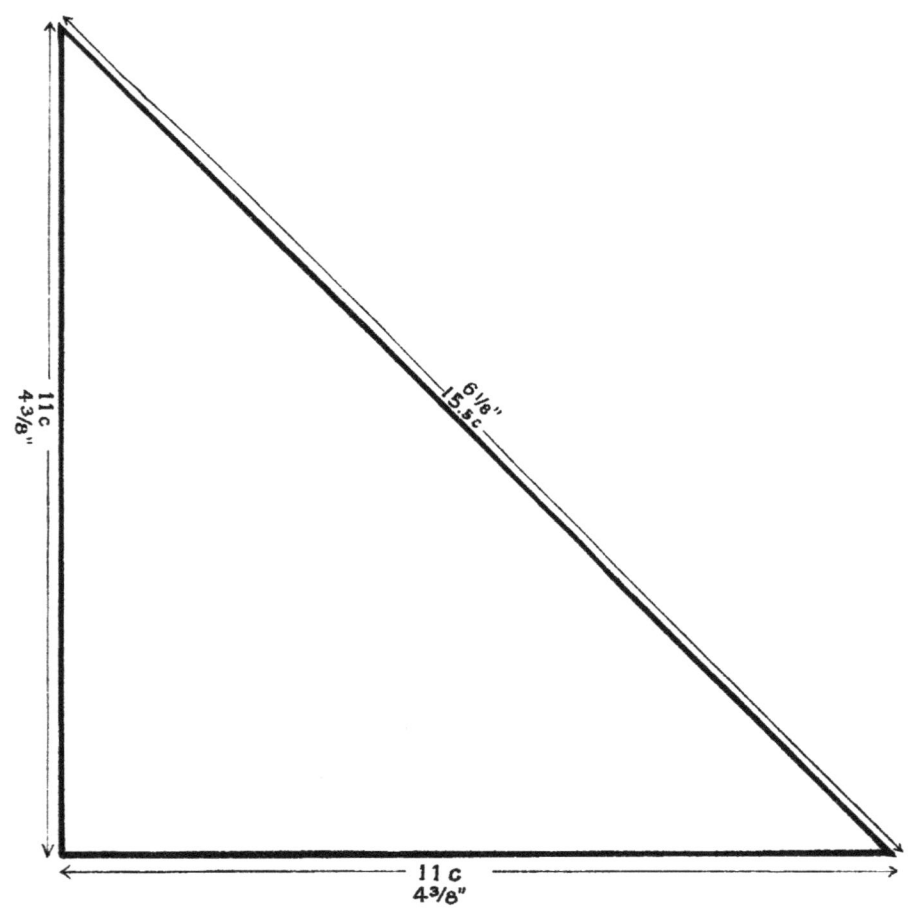

Full size of Model

MODEL No. 27

CANDLE SCREEN

28 c. x 12 c. (11 in. x 4 ¾ in.)

1. Cut out *three* pieces of cardboard similar to plan, 28 c. x 12 c. (11 in. x 4 ¾ in.), from bottom to base of triangular apex being 20.25 c. (8 in.).

2. Bind each piece.

3. Beginning at the bottom, and at a distance of 1 c. (3/8 in.) from edge, set off distances of 3 ½ c., 6 ½ c., 6 ½ c. (1 3/8 in., 2 5/8 in., 2 5/8 in.) on both the longer sides of one piece and on one long side only of each of the other two pieces.

4. At these points as centers, punch small holes.

5. Attach the three parts lightly by bows of colored ribbon.

CARDBOARD MODELLING

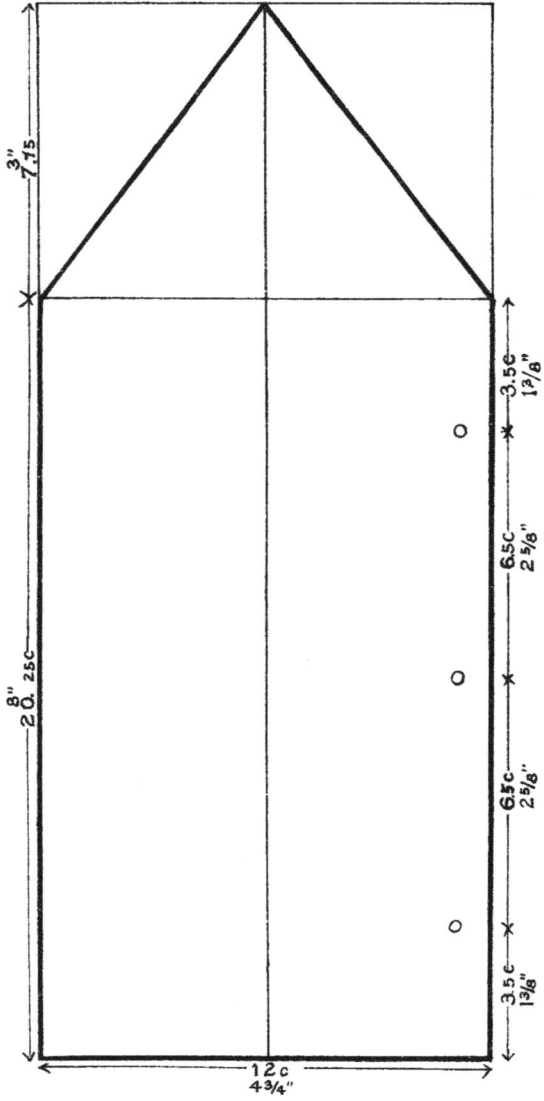

Half size of Model

MODEL No. 28

MUSIC PORTFOLIO—with flaps

35 c. x 25 c. (13 7/8 in. x 9 7/8 in.)

1. Cut out two oblongs *a, b*, each 35 c. x 25 c. (13 7/8 in. x 9 7/8 in.)

2. "*a*" must not be bound.

3. Bind *b* along each shorter side, and one long side.

4. Describe two oblongs each 25 c. x 10 c. (9 7/8 in. x 4 in.).

5. Along each short side set off 2.5 c. (1 in.) and set off from each angle opposite along long side 5 c. (2 in.).

6. Join these points across the angle, and cut out along these joining lines for sides *c, d*.

7. Bind all but the 25 c. edge.

8. For flap *e*, describe an oblong 35 c. x 10 c. (13 7/8 in. x 4 in.).

9. Set off on one long side a distance, from each end, of 5 c. (2 in.) and from opposite angles, along each short side, distances of 2.5 c. (1 in.).

10. Join these points across the angles, and cut out flap *e*.

11. Bind all but the 35 c. edge.

12. To 25 c. ends of oblong *a*, join *c* and *d* by strips of 5 c. (2 in.) wide cloth, allowing 3 c. between each edge, and binding overlapping 1 c. (3/8 in.) on each face. The ends of the 5 c. strips to fold inwards.

13. Cover the inner faces of these joins with brown enamel paper.

14. Join *a* and *b* in a similar manner, 5 c. strip and enamel paper inside.

15. Join *a* and *e* in a similar manner, 5 c. strip and enamel paper inside, as in Models 6 and 7.

CARDBOARD MODELLING

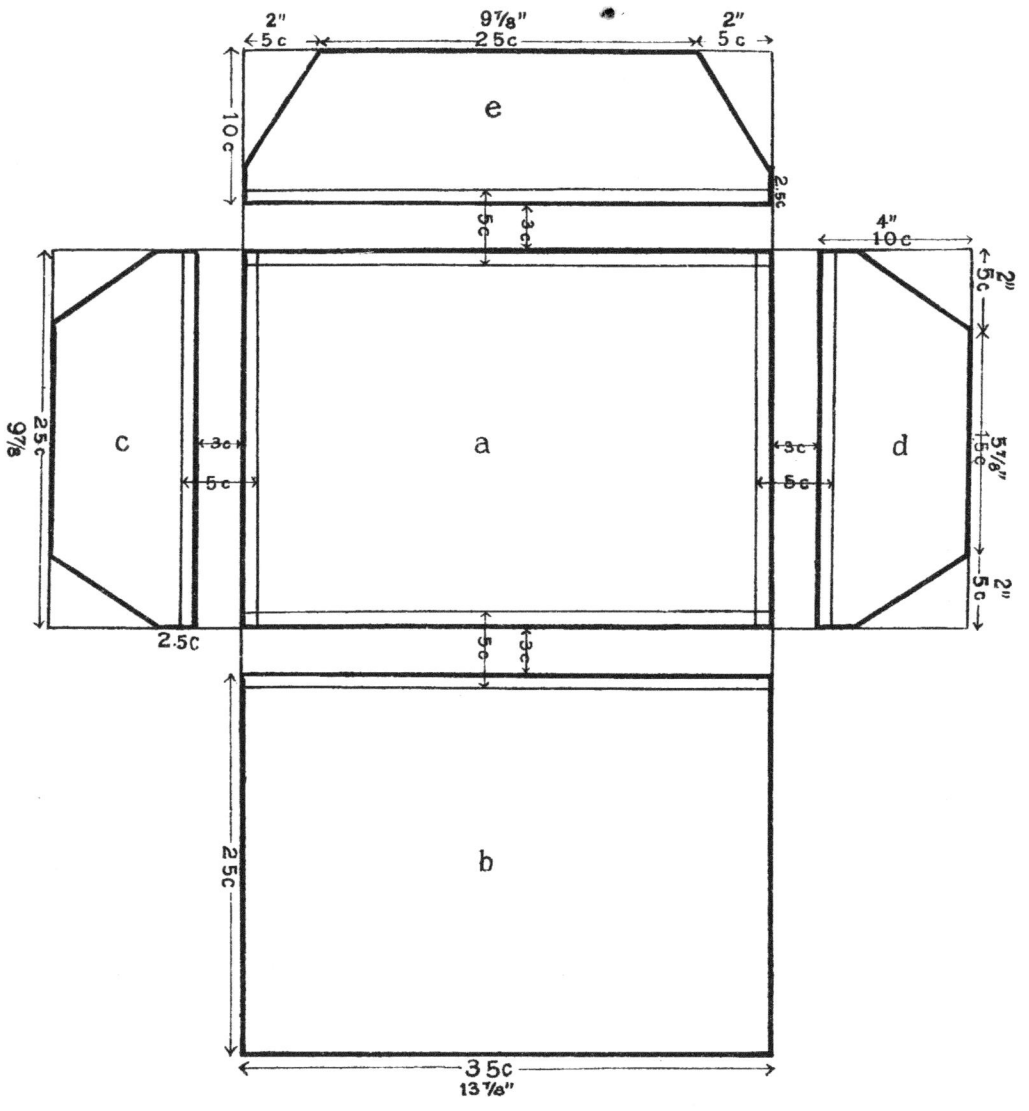

One fifth size of Model

MODEL No. 29

ALMANAC COVER

11.5 c. x 10 c. (4 ½ in. x 4 in.)

1. Cut two oblongs each 11.5 c. x 10 c. (4 ½ in. x 4 in.)

2. Join these by 3 c. (1 1/8 in.) strip of black binding, leaving 1 c. (3/8 in.) between the two, and overlapping at ends 1 c. (3/8 in.).

3. Cover the outside faces of which this join made with black cloth, folding over the inner faces 1 c., and leaving 1 c. between the two oblongs on outside.

4. Cover the inner face along the join with a black strip 3 c. wide, and reaching almost to the outside at each end.

5. Cover inside faces with red cloth or colored paper, leaving very small space of black round each oblong.

CARDBOARD MODELLING

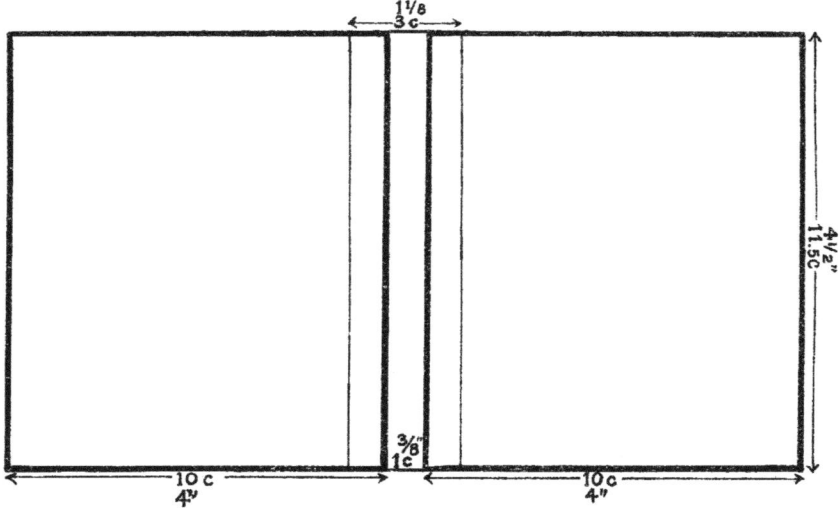

Half size of Model

MODEL No. 29a

DRAUGHT BOARD

26 c. x 26 c. (10 ¼ in. x 10 ¼ in.)

1. Describe a square of 26 c. (10 ¼ in.).

2. From each angle set off along each side 1 c. (3/8 in.) and join points so found by lines parallel to sides.

3. Join contiguous angles of the two squares.

4. Divide sides of inner square into eight parts of 3 c. (1 3/16 in.) each, and join across the square by lines parallel to the sides.

5. Cut out 32 squares of dark enamel paper, and 32 squares of lighter colored paper, each square 3 c. (1 3/16 in.) and fit as shown.

6. Cut strips of cardboard 1 c. (3/8 in.) wide, long edge 26 c. (10 ¼ in.), shorter edge 24 c. (9 ½ in.)

7. Cover these with binding on 24 c. edge, and one long face; glue to face of board so that binding on long sides overlaps back of board.

8. Cover back with enamel paper to within ½ c. of edge.

CARDBOARD MODELLING

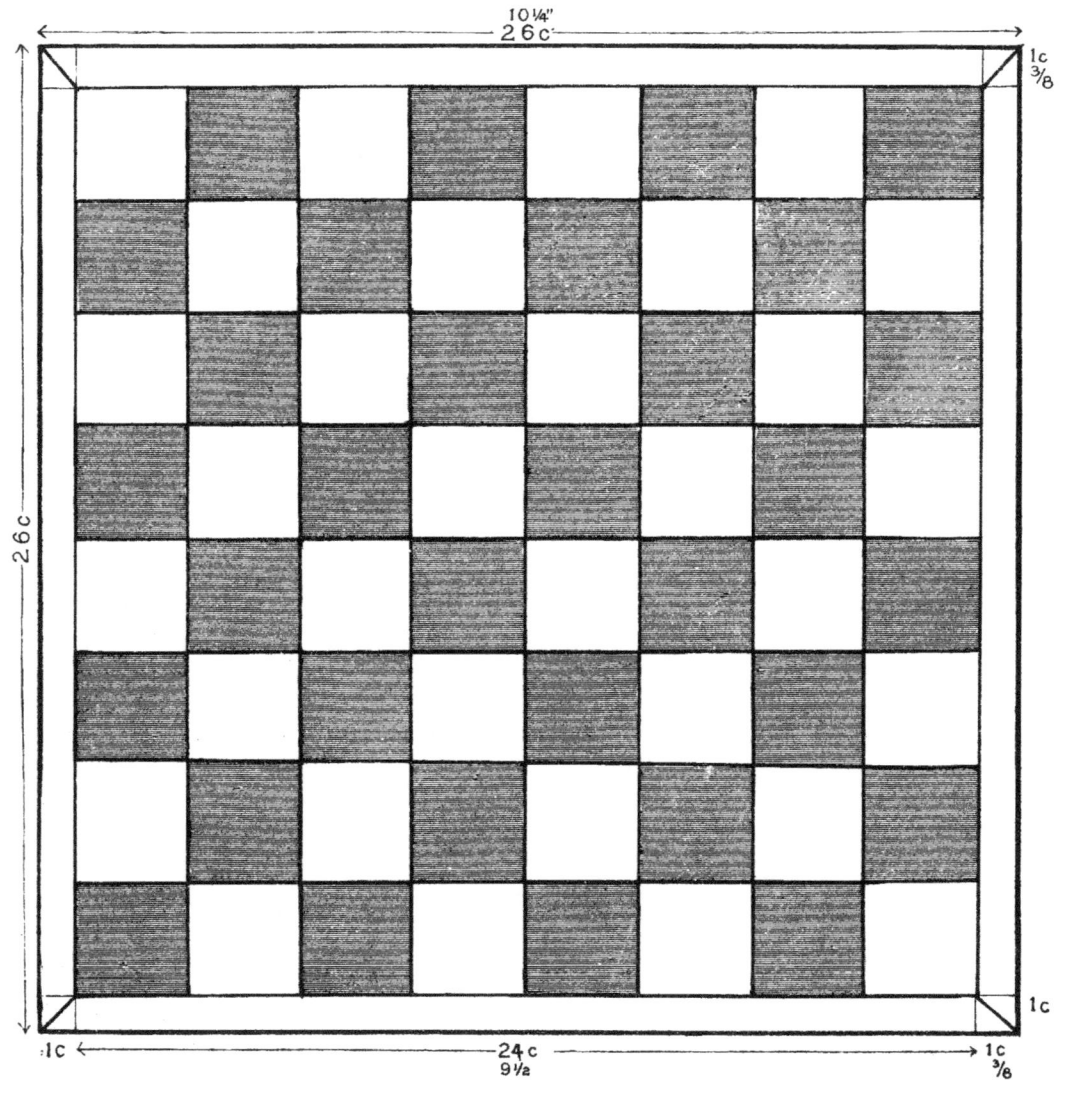

Half size of Model

MODEL No. 30

CARD CASE—*with pocket*

11 c. x 7 c. (4 3/8 in. x 2 ¾ in.)

1. Cut out two oblongs, each 11 c. x 7 c. (4 3/8 in. x 2 ¾ in.).

2. Join by a strip of black cloth 3 c. (1 1/8 in.) wide, leaving 1 c. (3/8 in.) between the two oblongs, and overlapping 1 c. at each end.

3. Cover the faces on which the join is made with black cloth, folding over the inner faces 1 c. (3/8 in.) and leaving 1 c. between the two oblongs on the outside.

4. Cover inner side of joining strip with another black cloth strip covering 1 c. (3/8 in.) of each inner face, and reaching almost to the outside at each end.

5. Cover each inner face with red or other colored cloth, leaving a very small strip of black along each edge.

6. Cut out an oblong *ABCD* of red cloth (or cloth of similar color to the lining of the backs) 16.5 c. x 13.5 c. (6 ½ in. x 5 5/16 in.).

7. Set off as shown in drawing of the pocket 3 c. (1 1/8 in.) from each end of *AB*, and draw lines across the diagonal parallel to *AD* and *BC*.

8. Draw *EF* 7 c. (2 5/8 in.) from *AB*, and *GH* 1 c. (3/8 in.) from *DC*.

9. Along *EF* set off three successive distances of 1 c. (3/8 in.) from each end, and draw lines (dotted) perpendicular to *GH*.

10. Cut out along thickened lines.

11. The dotted lines are the lines of folding. Fold strip formed by line *GH* along *GH*, and glue securely; this forms a firm edge for the front of the pocket.

12. Fold along *ab* inwards as with *GH*. (No 11)

13. Fold along *cd* the opposite way so as to form accordion ends.

14. Fold along *ef* as with *GH* and *ab*.

15. Fold along *EF* inwards, so as to bring the double edge of *GH* nearly to *AB*.

16. Bring the strips formed by *ab* behind the sides *ge*, and fasten securely.

17. Fasten the whole securely over the colored face of one of the covers, with the mouth of the pocket to the hinge of the case.

CARDBOARD MODELLING

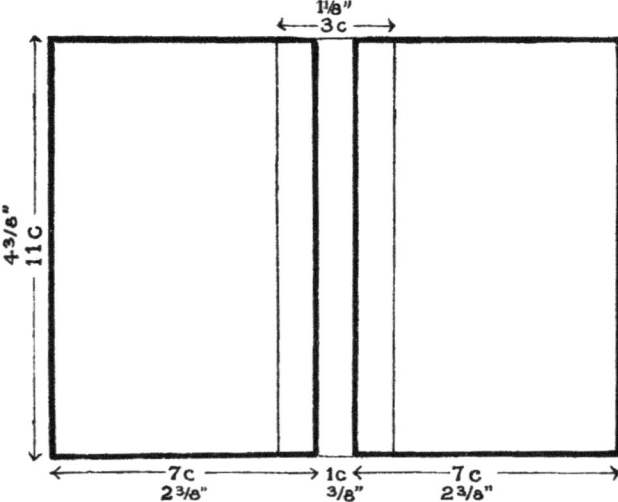

Plan of Pocket.

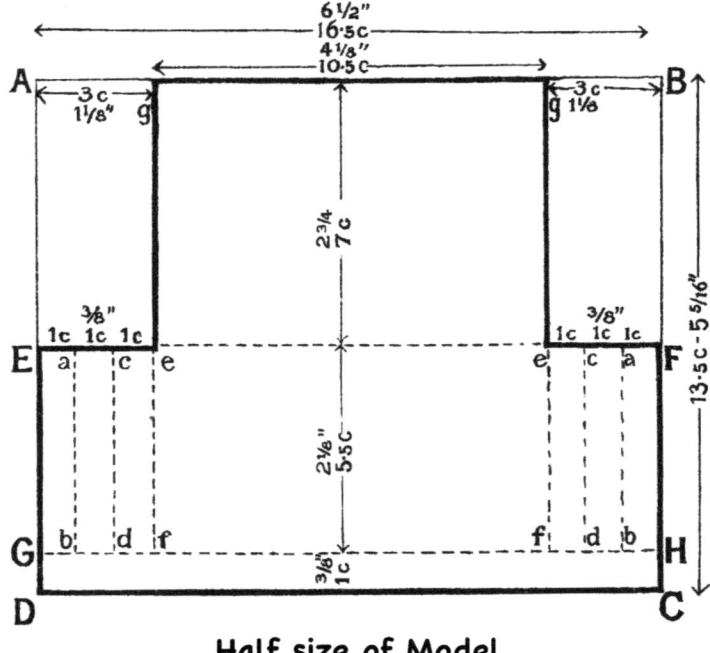

Half size of Model

MODEL No. 30*a*

POCKET CASE—*with pencil slot*

21 c. x 9 c. (8 ¼ in. x 3 ½ in.)

1. Cut out two oblongs of cardboard, each 21 c. x 9 c. (8 ¼ in. x 3 ½ in.).

2. Join these by a strip of cloth 3 c. (1 1/8 in.) wide and 23 c. (9 1/16 in.) long, leaving 1 c. (3/8 in.) between the two oblongs, and overlapping 1 c. (3/8 in.) at each end.

3. Cover the faces of which joining strip is fixed with black cloth, folding over the inner faces on three sides, 1 c. (3/8 in.), each sheet of cloth to be cut 23 c x 10 c. (9 1/16 in. x 4 in.).

4. Cut out a piece of black cloth 6 c. x 5 c. (2 3/8 in. x 2 in.).

5. Fold over 1 c. along each long side, and fasten down so as to make a double edge in each case.

6. Double so as to bring the two raw edges together, and fasten them securely.

7. Fix this loop as in drawing, leaving half the width outside the oblong.

8. Cover inner side of the hinge strip with a strip of cloth 3 c. wide.

9. Cover inner face of each board with red cloth, leaving 1 c. along the hinge strip and a very narrow space along each of the other edges.

CARDBOARD MODELLING

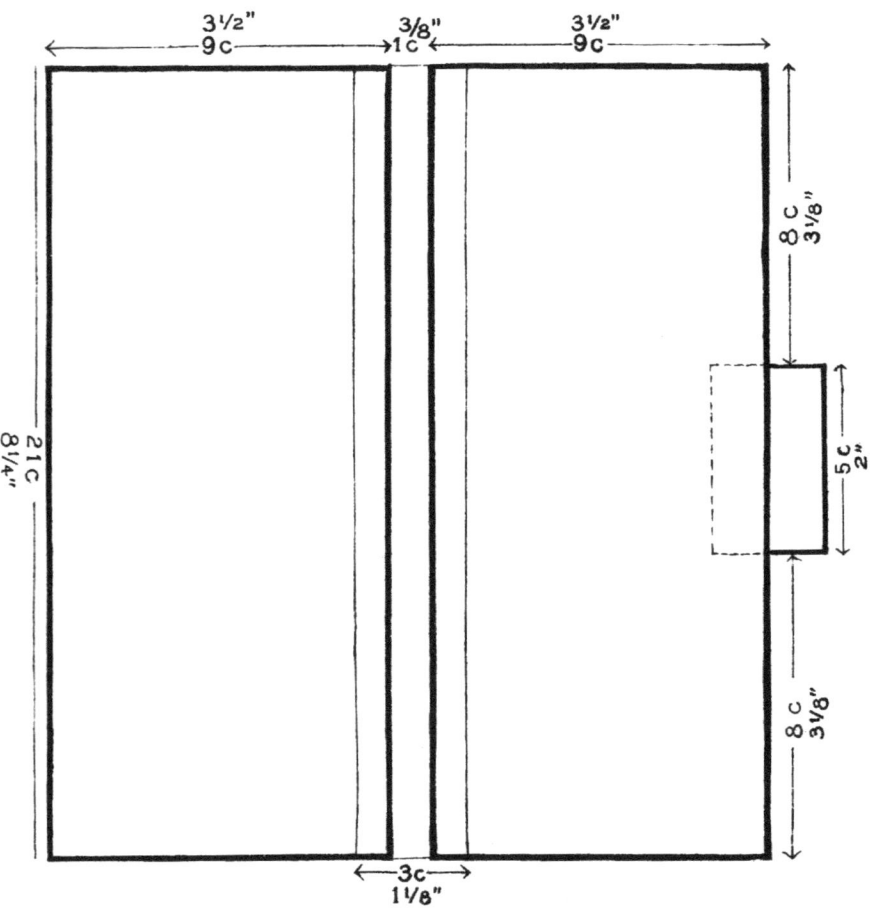

Half size of Model

MODEL No. 31

CUBICAL MONEY BOX

7 c. x 7 c. x 7 c. (2 ¾ in. x 2 ¾ in. x 2 ¾ in.)

1. Describe an oblong 28 c. x 21 c. (11 in. x 2 ¾ in.)

2. Set off distances of 7 c. (2 ¾ in.) along each side, and draw lines across the oblong from these points parallel to the sides.

3. Cut out along the thickened lines.

4. Cut half or three-parts through along the dotted lines, all on the same side.

5. At a distance of 1.5 c. (5/8 in.) from *a* and *b* along the center line, punch small holes.

6. Cut out narrow slit connecting these two holes.

7. Bend backward from the half cuts, making the square *c, d, f, e* the base of the box, and fit the corners.

8. Bind perpendicular corners.

9. Bind outside upper and lower edges.

CARDBOARD MODELLING

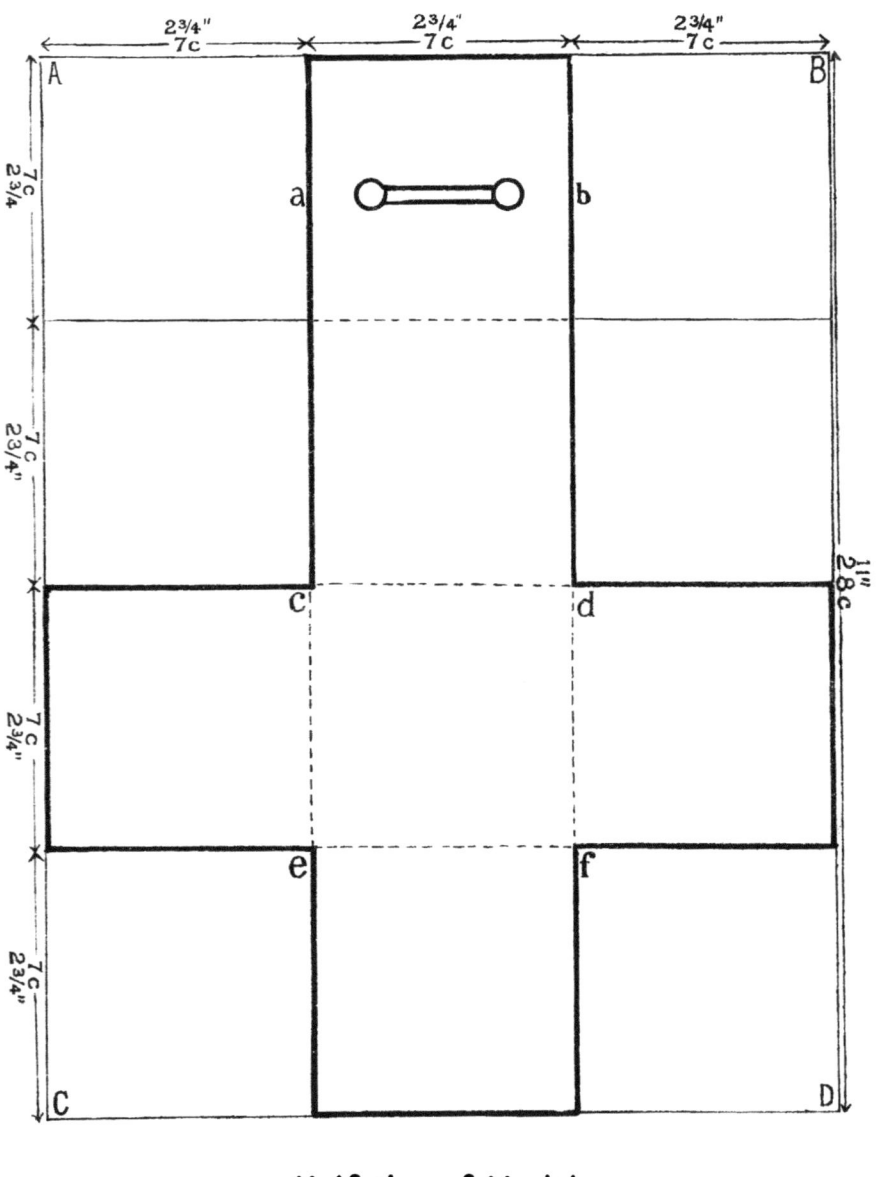

Half size of Model

99

MODEL No. 32 (*a, b, c, d*)
FOUR SILK WINDERS

(*a*) 4 c. (1 5/8 in.) square (*c*) 6 c. x 5 c. (2 3/8 in. x 2 in.)

(*b*) 6 c. x 5 c. (2 3/8 in. x 2 in.) (*d*) 5.5 c. (2 3/16 in.) square

32a. 1. Describe a square of 4 c. (1 5/8 in.)

2. From the center of each side draw lines across the square.

3. From the center of each side set off 8 m. (5/16 in.) towards center of the square.

4. Join these points with the angles of the square, and cut out.

5. Bind the edges as shown by fine lines within the thick ones.

32b. 1. Describe a square *ABCD* of 6 c. (2 3/8 in.). Find the center and describe a concentric circle of 2 c. (3/4 in.)

2. From the centers of sides draw lines across the square parallel to the sides.

3. Describe a hexagon within the circle, having two of its angles upon the horizontal diameter of the circle.

4. Set off along *AB* and *CD* distances of 0.5 c. (3/16 in.), and draw lines *ac, bd* from these points.

5. On *ac, bd* set off distances of 1.5 c. (5/8 in.) from each end, and join these points with the angles of the inscribed hexagon.

6. Cut out along the thickened lines and bind the edges, leaving triangular spaces at the inner angles as shown in the drawing.

32c. 1. Describe an oblong 5 c. x 6 c. (2 in. x 2 3/8 in.)

2. *Bisect* the 5 c. (2 in.) sides, and *trisect* the 6 c. (2 3/8 in.) sides.

3. Join *ab, ac, de, df.*

4. Cut out along the thickened lines, and bind as in *32 (a, b)*.

CARDBOARD MODELLING

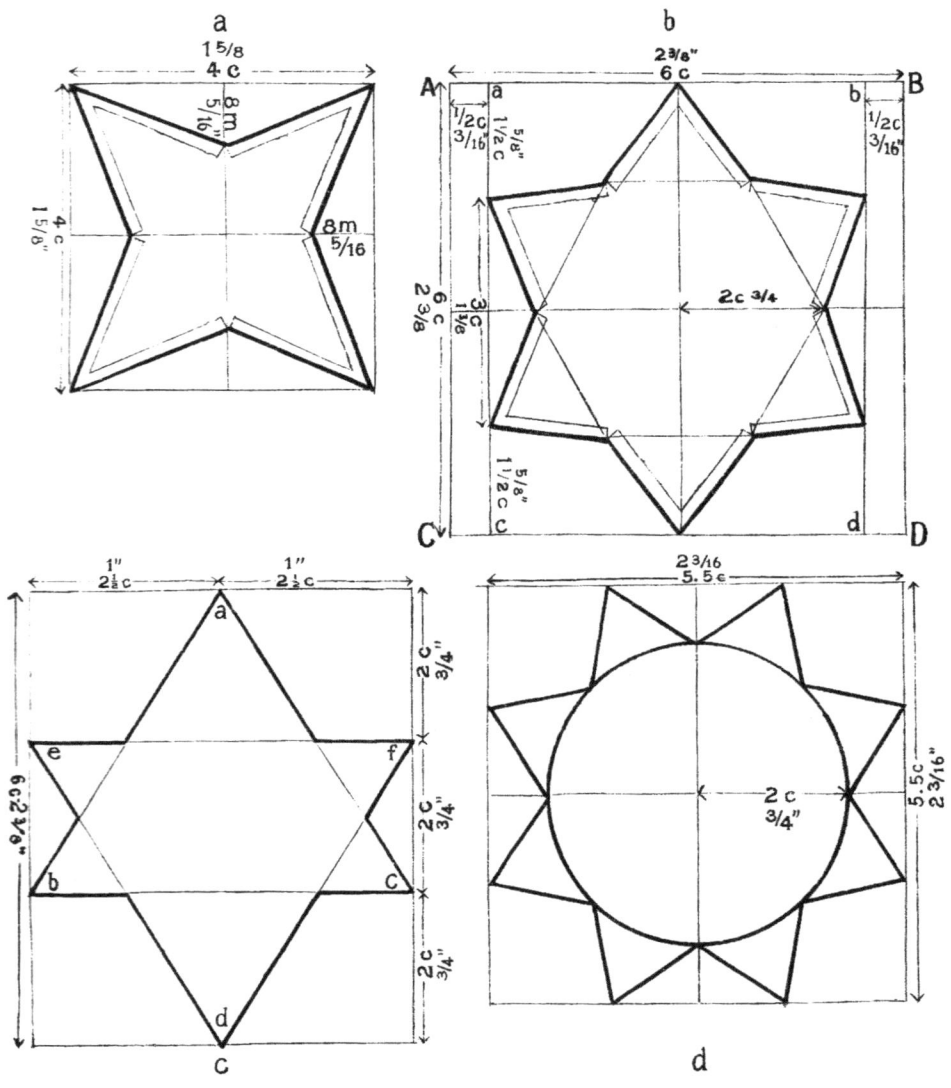

Size as Model

32d. 1. Describe a square of 5.5 c. (2 3/16 in.)

2. Draw diagonals, and with half of one diagonal set off distances from each angle along each side. The points thus found are the angles of an inscribed octagon.

3. With the same center inscribe a circle of 2 c. (3/4 in.) radius.

4. Draw lines across the square parallel to the sides from the center of each side.

5. Join the points where these parallel lines and diagonals cut the circle with the points found in Direction 2 and the centers of the sides.

6. Cut out along the thickened lines, and bind as in 32*a*.

MODEL No. 33

CIRCULAR MAT

6 c. radius (2 3/8 in.)

1. Describe a circle of 6 c. (2 3/8 in.) radius.

2. Cut out this circle.

3. Bind round the edge; while the binding is moist, stretch it with some force—it will then fit evenly without creases or overlapping.

4. Cut out a circle of 5 ½ c. (2 ¼ in.) in brown enamel paper, and cover one face within ¼ c. of the edge.

5. Cut out a similar circle of red morocco paper, and cover the other face in the same manner.

Any two other contrasting colors may be used.

NOTE: The faces might be covered before the binding is done, if preferred; in this case the covering paper would be of the same size as the Model.

CARDBOARD MODELLING

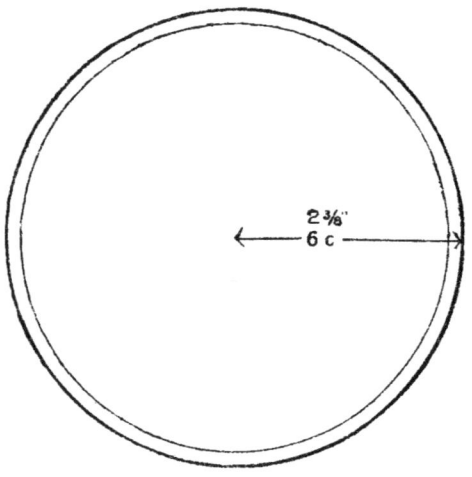

Half size of Model

MODEL No. 34

TWELVE-CORNERED MAT

10 c. (4 in.) radius

1. Describe a circle of 10 c. (4 in.) radius.

2. Inscribe a hexagon, by setting off the radius along the circumference.

3. Bisect one of the arcs of the circle thus formed.

4. From this bisection set off similar distances to those in Direction No. 2.

5. From each of these points draw lines to the third point.

6. From each point thus obtained in the circumference, draw lines to the nearest points of intersection.

7. Cut out along the thickened lines.

8. Bind as in No. 32, leaving open space at each inner angle.

CARDBOARD MODELLING

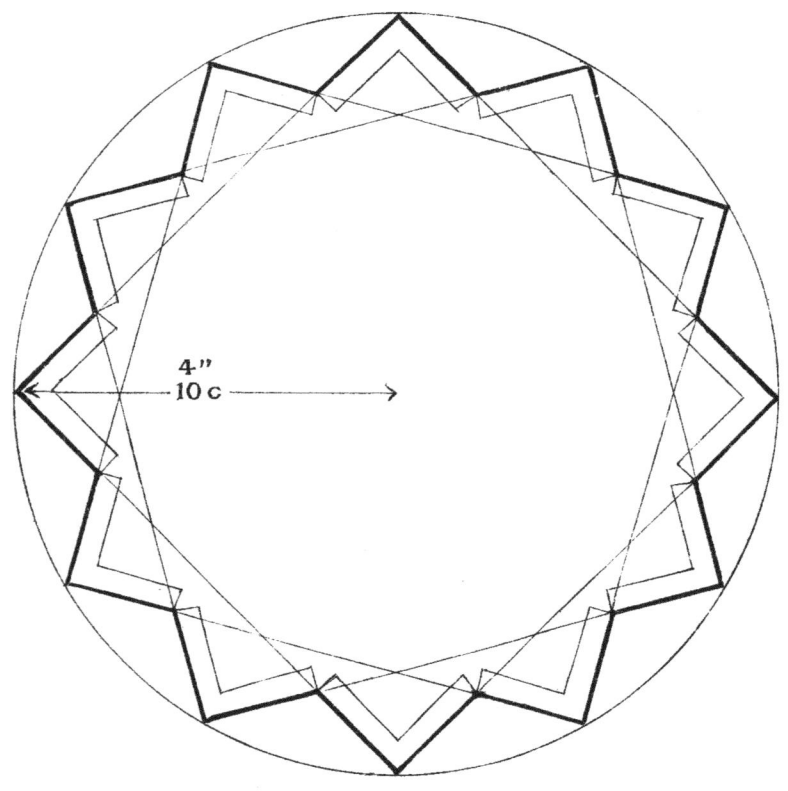

Half size of Model

MODEL No. 35

SQUARE TRAY—*with rectangular divisions*

10 c. x 10 c. x 2 c. (4 in. x 4 in. x ¾ in.)

1. Describe a square of 14 c. (5 ½ in.)

2. Set off from each angle distances of 2 c. (3/4 in.) along each side.

3. Join these points across the square by lines drawn parallel to the sides.

4. Cut out the whole square and then through along the thickened lines.

5. Cut half or three parts through along the dotted lines.

6. Bend sides backwards from the half-cuts, and fit neatly at the angles.

7. Bind (i.) outside perpendicular corners, (ii.) upper edge, (iii.) outside lower edge.

8. Cut out two strips of cardboard each 10 c. x 2 c. (4 in. x ¾ in.)

9. Cut out of the center of each a slit the width of the thickness of the board. In one slit the cut will be as shown in darker lines at *a*, in the other at the top, as shown by dotted lines at *b*.

10. Bind strips along the top edge.

11. Fit into the Tray along the thin bisecting lines, and fix with a touch of glue.

CARDBOARD MODELLING

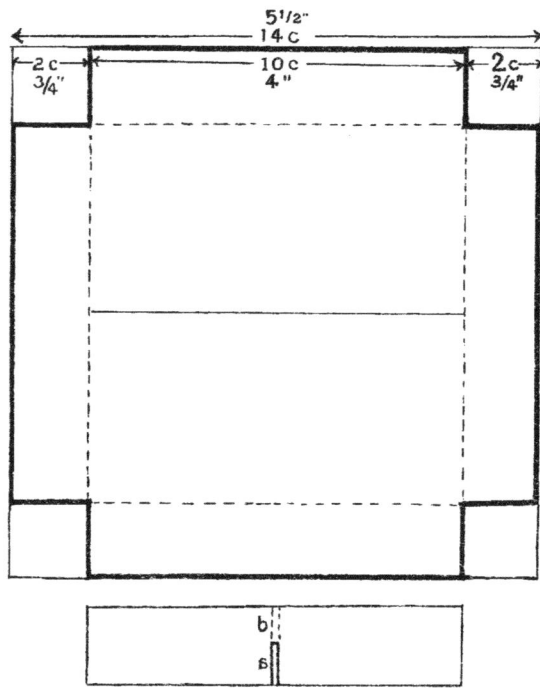

Half size of Model

MODEL No. 35a

SQUARE TRAY—*with diagonal divisions*

13.5 c. (5 ¼ in.) UPPER EDGE

9 c. (3 ½ in.) LOWER EDGE

3 c. (1 3/16 in.) SIDES

1. Describe a square of 15 c. (5 7/8 in.)

2. Set off, from the angles, along each side, distances of 3 c. (1 3/16 in.), and draw lines from these points parallel to the sides of the square.

3. From each angle of the outer square set off along each side distances of 0.75 c. (5/16 in.), and join these points with the adjacent angles of the square.

4. Cut out along the thick lines, and half or three parts through along the dotted lines.

5. Bend back from the half-cuts, and fit the corners neatly.

6. Bind (i.) outside corners, (ii.) inside corners, (iii.) upper edge, (iv.) outer lower edge, (v.) inside lower edge.

7. Cut out two 3 c. (1 3/16 in.) strips of board—upper edge the length of diagonal edge to edge, lower edge of strips equal to diagonal of base of Tray.

8. Cut out and bind as in No. 35, and fix along diagonals.

CARDBOARD MODELLING

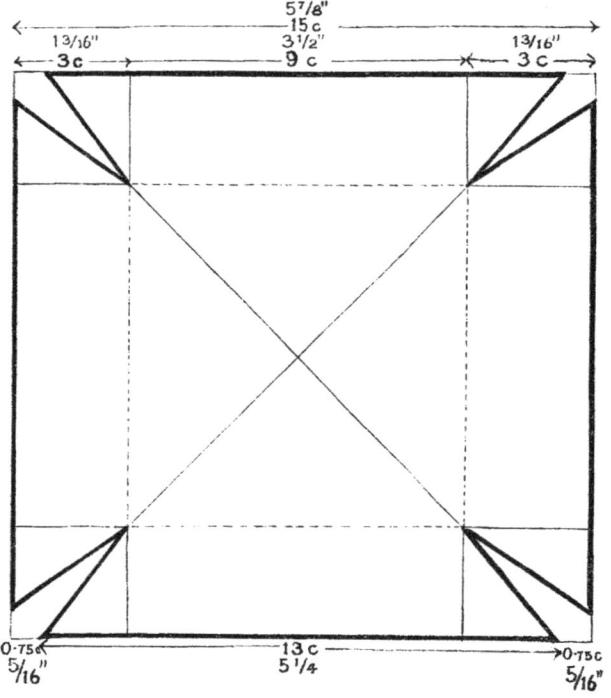

Half size of Model

MODEL No. 36

PYRAMIDAL WATCH STAND

BASE 12 c. (4 ¾ in.) SIDES 16 c. (6 ¼ in.)

1. Describe an isosceles triangle *ABC*, having base 12 c. (4 ¾ in.) and sides 16 c. (6 ¼ in.)

2. With *A* and *B* as centers, and radius of 12 c. (4 ¾ in.) describe arcs at D, D_1, D_2, and with *C* as center and radius of 16 c (6 ¼ in.) describe arcs intersecting at D_1, D_2.

3. Join AD, BD, CD_1, CD_2.

4. At *E*, and on the opposite face of *ABC* to the half-cuts, glue firmly a thin piece of wood or stout board, and bore a hole for hook.

5. With *F*, 6 c. (2 3/8 in.) from the base along the center line, as center, describe a circle of 2.5 c. (1 in.) radius.

6. Cut out along thickened lines, and half or three parts through along dotted lines.

7. Bend backwards from the lines of half-cuts, and fit so that D, D_1, and D_2 meet.

8. Bind outside lines of juncture, and half-cuts.

9. Cut out a circular piece of cardboard, radius 2.5 c. (1 in.), and cover one face with colored paper or cloth.

10. Cut out a 1 c. (3/8 in.) strip of cardboard, and cover both faces and one edge with black cloth.

11. While moist, bend this strip so as to fit round the outside of the circular piece in Direction No. 9, the latter to have its covered face toward the inside of this circumscribing edge. Glue the two firmly together, leaving a short distance between the two ends of the edge strip.

12. When quite set glue firmly into position shown by the circle on the plan, with the open space in the edge strip on the top side towards *E*.

13. At *E* screw in a small brass hook through hole bored in Direction No. 4.

CARDBOARD MODELLING

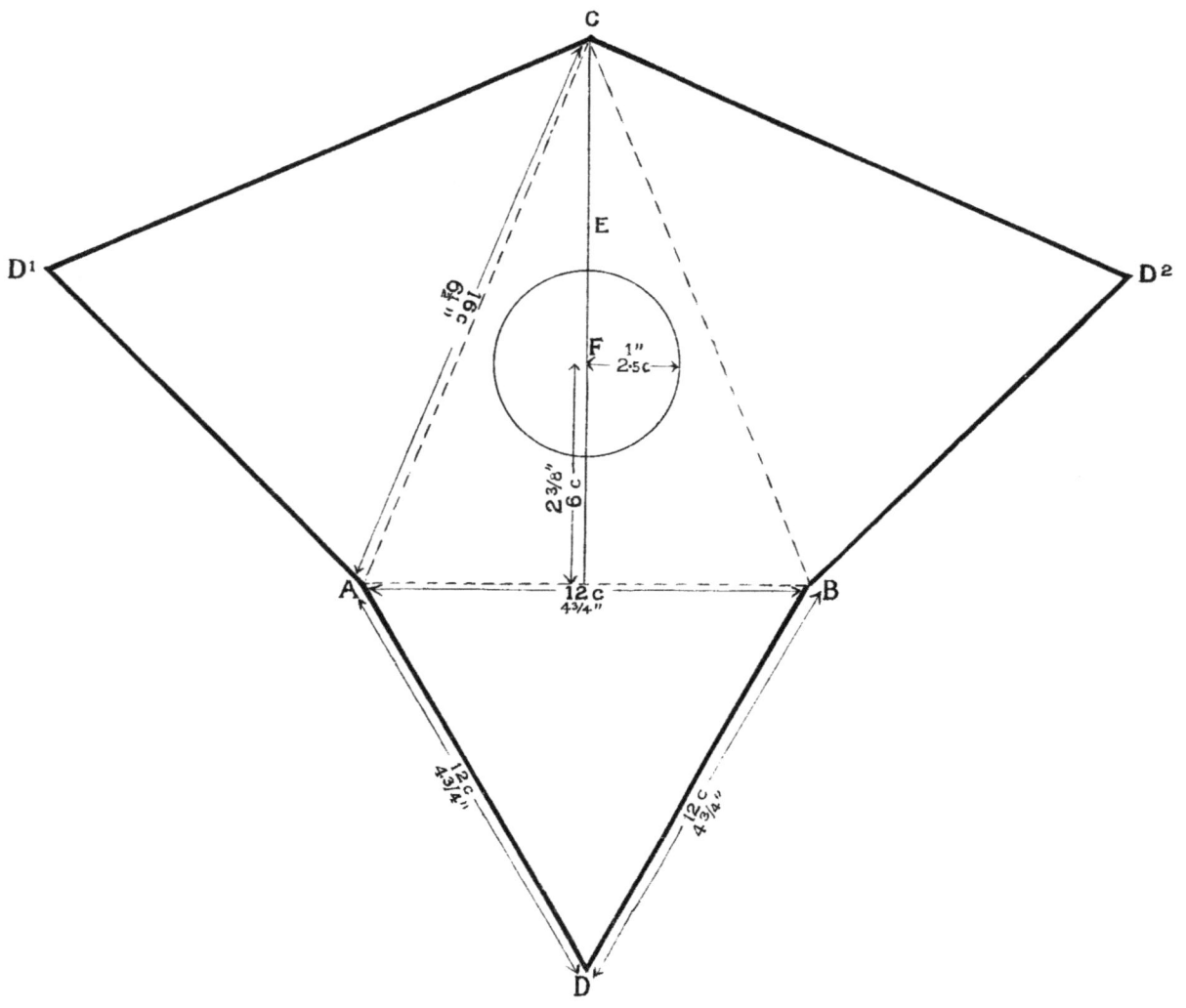

Half size of Model

MODEL No. 37

OBLONG TRAY—*with sloping sides and projecting base*

UPPER EDGE 17 c. x 14.5 c. (6 ¾ in. x 5 ¾ in.)
BASE 12.5 c. x 10 c. (5 in. x 4 in.)
SIDES 3 c. (1 1/8 in.)

PROJECTING BASE 13.5 c. x 11 c. (5 3/8 in. x 4 3/8 in.)

1. Describe an oblong 18.5 c. x 16 c. (7 ¼ in. x 6 ¼ in.)

2. From each angle set off along each side distances of 3 c. (1 1/8 in.); join these points across the oblong by lines parallel to sides

3. From each angle set off along each side distances of 0.75 c. (5/16 in.), and join with the adjacent angles of the inner oblong.

4. Cut out along the thickened lines, and half or three parts through along the dotted lines.

5. Bend sides backwards from the cuts, and fit neatly at the angles.

6. Bind (i.) outside corners, (ii.) inside corners, (iii.) upper edge in one strip, (iv.) outside edge along half-cuts, (v.) inside lower edge.

7. Cut out an oblong 13.5 c. x 11 c. (5 3/8 in. x 4 3/8 in.)

8. Bind, and glue firmly outside base so as to project ½ c. (3/16 in.) on each side.

CARDBOARD MODELLING

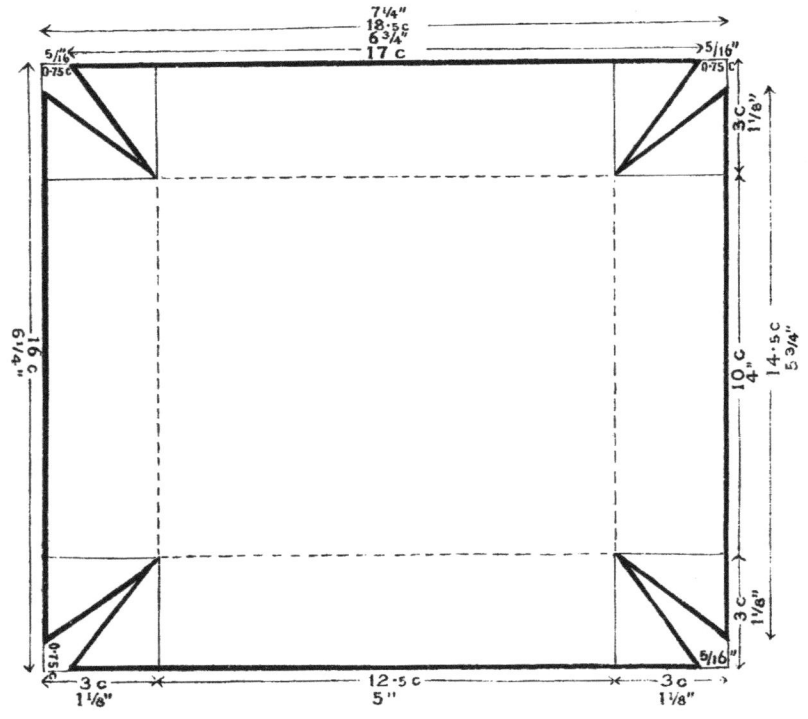

Half size of Model

MODEL No. 38

MENU TABLET

17 c. x 12 c. (6 ¾ in. x 4 ¾ in.)

1. Describe an oblong 18.5 c. x 13.5 c. (7 ¼ in. x 5 3/8 in.)

2. From each angle set off distances of 0.75 c. (5/16 in.) along each side, and draw lines through these points parallel to sides.

3. At each angle set off distances of 1.5 c. (5/8 in.) and complete squares of 1.5 c. in each angle.

4. From inner angles of these squares as centers, and with 1.5 c. as radius, describe arcs of circles touching each of the two adjacent sides of the oblong, and cutting lines formed in Direction No. 2. These arcs and lines form the outside edge of the model.

5. Bind the edges, stretching the binding while moist to fit neatly round the curves, and joining neatly in the angles.

6. Cut a piece of card 13 c. x 8 c. (5 1/8 in. x 3 1/8 in.) and to this affix a strip of cloth 7 c. x 5 c. (2 ¾ in. x 2 in.) folded double lengthwise, allowing half of the strip to project from the long side of the card.

7. To the opposite face of this board, glue along close to the edge a similar oblong of tablet writing-glass.

8. Bind the board and glass round the edges with black cloth, which should cover 1 c. (3/8 in.) of the glass on each side of the front face.

9. Glue this board firmly into position shown by the 13 c. x 8 c. oblong.

CARDBOARD MODELLING

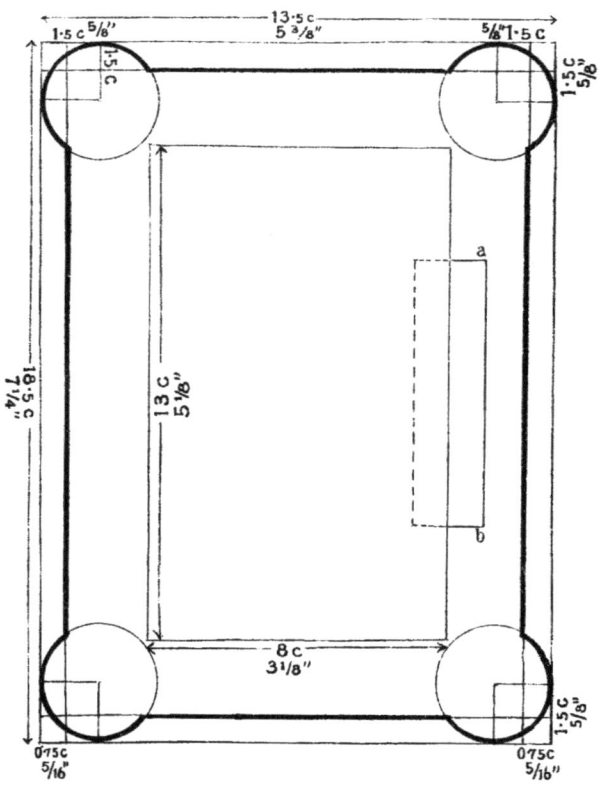

MODEL No. 39
WALL POCKET
26 c. x 20 c. (10 ¼ in. x 7 7/8 in.)

1. Describe an oblong (Fig. 1) 26 c. x 20 c. (10 ¼ in. x 7 7/8 in.)
2. From each end of the long sides set off distances of 2 c., 4 c. (3/4 in., 1 5/8 in.) and join across the oblong.
3. From the top of the short sides set off distances of 2 c., 1 c., 4 c., 2 c. (3/4 in., 3/8 in., 1 5/8 in., ¾ in.) and join across the oblong.
4. From a and a' set off along line aa' distances from each end of 1 c. (3/8 in.) and join with bb'.
5. Join x and x' to c and c' respectively.
6. From the 4 c. distances on top long side set off towards the center of the side distances of 2 c. (3/4 in.) and join with the points where line aa' cuts the 4 c. lines.
7. Cut out along the thick lines, and bind the edges.
8. Describe an oblong 24 c. x 18 c. (9 ½ in. x 7 1/8 in.)
9. From each angle set off along each side distances of 4 c. (1 5/8 in.) and join across the oblong.
10. From each angle of the inner oblong set off along each side distances of 1 c. (3/8 in.) and join across each angle.
11. From each side set off along each 4 c. line distances of 1 c. (3/8 in.) and join the points along each side.
12. Cut out along the thick lines, and bind all the cut edges.
13. Cut out an oblong of stiff blue or red paper 21 c. x 31 c. (8 ¼ in. x 12 1/16 in.).
14. Fold this oblong to form a pocket 21 c x 15 ½ c.
15. Cut two strips of cloth 16 c. x 6 c. (6 5/16 in. x 2 3/8 in.)
16. Fold these strips in two longitudinally, and each long side 1 c. (3/8 in.) backwards.
17. Glue the 1 c. folds to the sides of the folded paper so as to form the ends of the pocket, with the central fold within.
18. Glue one face of the pocket to the front face of the cardboard (Fig. 2) and the other face to the back (Fig. 1).

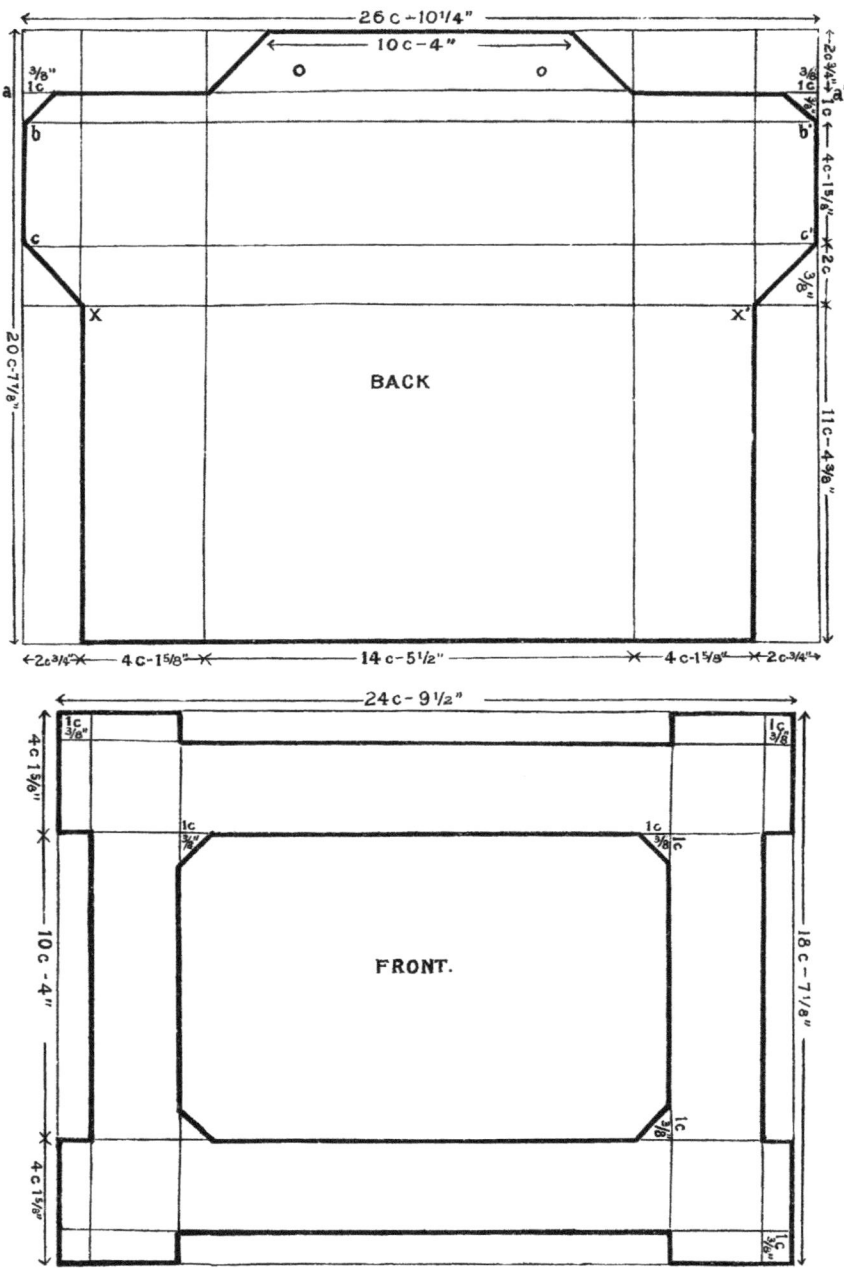

Half size of Model

117

MODEL No. 40

SLIDING PEN BOX

DRAWER 20 c. X 5.5 c. x 3 c. (7 7/8 in. x 2 1/8 in. x 1 3/16 in.)

COVER 20 c. x 6 c. x 3.5 c. (7 7/8 in. x 2 3/8 in. x 1 3/8 in.)

1. Describe an oblong 26 c. x 11.5 c. (10 ¼ in. x 4 ½ in.)
2. From each angle set off along each side distances of 3 c. (1 3/16 in.) and join the points across the oblong.
3. Cut out along the thick lines, and half or three parts through along dotted lines.
4. Bend back from the half cuts, and bind outside corners.
5. Bind upper edge.
6. Bind outside lower edge.
7. Describe an oblong 20 c. x 19 c. (7 7/8 in. x 7 ½ in.).
8. Along the shorter sides set off distances of 3.5 c., 6 c., 3.5 c., and 6 c. (1 3/8 in., 2 3/8 in., 1 3/8 in., and 2 3/8 in.).
9. Join these points across the oblong.
10. Cut out along the thick lines, and half or three parts through along the dotted lines.
11. Bend backwards from the half-cuts and fit neatly.
12. Bind along line where the two cut edges meet.
13. Bind outside lines of half-cuts.
14. Bind the ends, each with one strip.

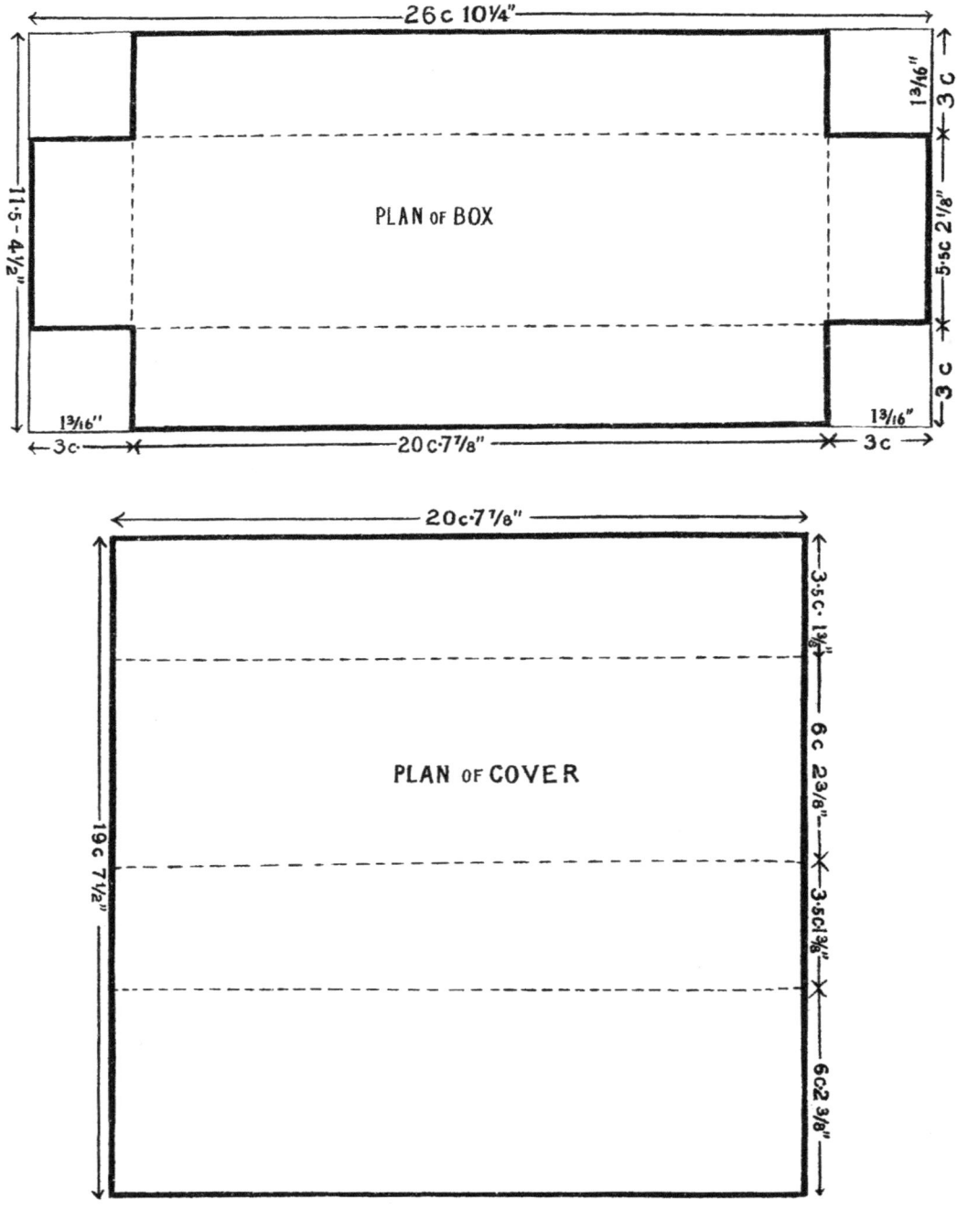

Half size of Model

MODEL No. 41

CUBICAL BOX—*with hinge lid and double sides and lid*

6 c. x 6 c. x 6 c. (2 3/8 in.)

1. Describe a square of 18 c. (7 1/8 in.)

2. On each side set off distances of 6 c. (2 3/8 in.)

3. Join the opposite points.

4. Cut out along the thick lines, and half or three parts through along the dotted lines.

5. Bend sides backwards from half-cuts, and bind outside perpendicular angle of the cube.

6. Bind (i.) upper edge, (ii.) outside lower edge.

7. Cut out a square of 6.5 c. (2 9/16 in.) for lid, and bind.

8. Cut out a square of 5.75 c. (2 ½ in.) and bind.

9. Glue the latter square firmly on No. 8 at equal distances from each side, inserting a projecting tag of 1 c. (3/8 in.) cloth between the two and in the center of a side.

10. Join the lid to the upper edge of one side of the box by a 4 c. (1 ½ in.) strip of cloth, leaving 2 c. (1 ¾ in.) on the outside of each.

11. Describe a similar figure in cardboard to the one shown in drawing—dimensions 17.25 c. (6 ¾ in.) square, with distances from each angle of 5.75 c. (2 ¼ in.). Cut out and bind outer edge of each wing. Bend back along lines of half-cuts, and fit within the box.

CARDBOARD MODELLING

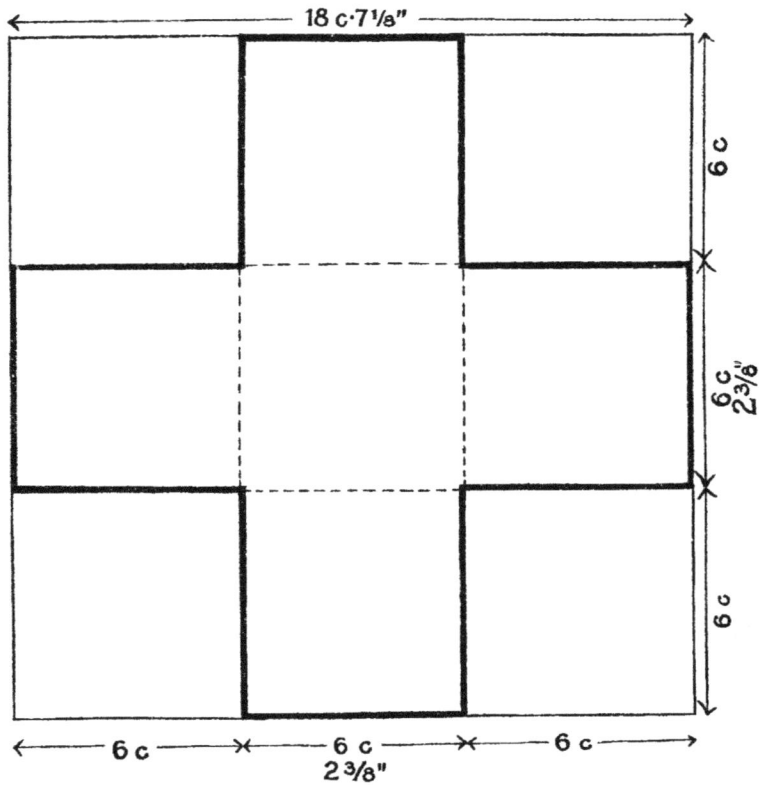

Half size of Model

MODEL No. 42

HEXAGONAL TRAY—*with sloping sides and curved edges*

4 c. x 10 c. (1 5/8 in. x 4 in.)

1. Describe a circle with 4 c. (1 5/8 in.) radius.

2. Inscribe a hexagon by setting off the radius along the circumference.

3. With same center describe a circle of 9 c. (3 ½ in.) radius.

4. Through the opposite angles of the hexagon draw lines to this outer circle fixing angles of outer hexagon.

5. From each of these points set off on each side along the circumference a distance of 0.75 c. (5/16 in.).

6. Join these points with the adjacent angle of the inner hexagon.

7. With the middle point of each side of the inner hexagon as center, describe arcs touching each of the points found in Direction No. 5.

8. Cut out along the thick lines, and half or three parts through along the dotted lines.

9. Bend sides back from the half-cuts, and fit neatly.

10. Bind (i.) outside angles, (ii.) inside angles, (iii.) upper edge, (iv.) outer lower edge, (v.) inside lower edge.

Note: In No. 8 cut *from* the angles of the inner hexagon *to* the outer edge.

CARDBOARD MODELLING

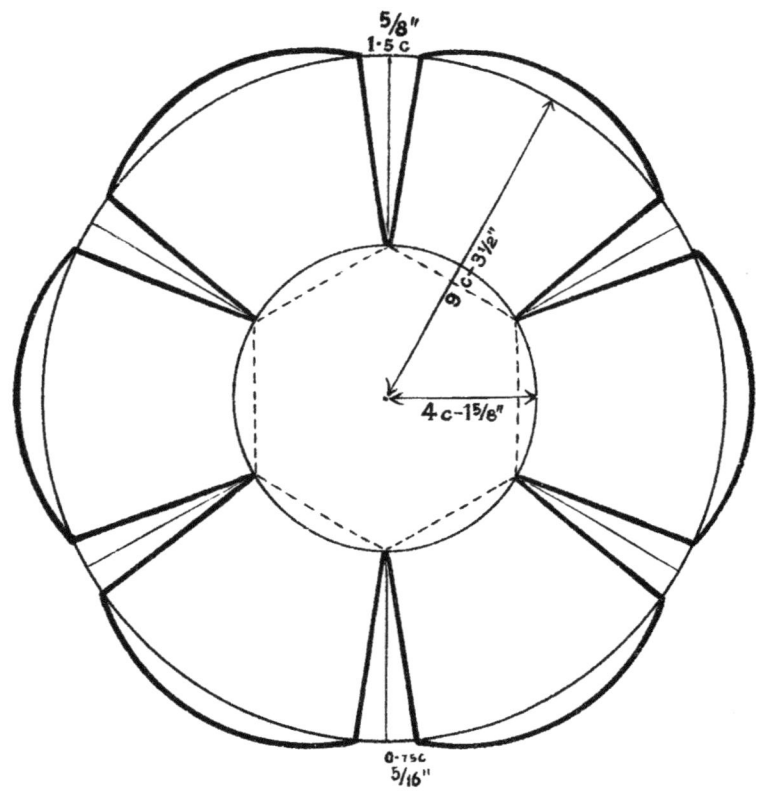

Half size of Model

MODEL No. 43

HEXAGONAL SHELF OR WALL POCKET

17 c. x 7 c. x 11 c. (6 5/8 in. x 2 ¾ in. x 4 3/8 in.)

1. Describe an oblong 18 c. x 17 c. (7 1/8 in. x 6 5/8 in.) (Fig. 1).

2. Along each 18 c. (7 1/8 in.) side of the oblong from the top, set off distances of 2 c., 4 c., 5 c., 4 c., 3 c., (3/4 in., 1 5/8 in., 2 in., 1 5/8 in., 1 1/8 in.) and draw lines across the oblong parallel to the shorter sides.

3. On the top short side set off from each angle distances of 3 c. (1 1/8 in.) and 5.5 c. (2 3/16 in.) and from the 3 c. distances drop perpendiculars to the first cross line.

4. On the lower short side set off from each angle distances of 2 c. (3/4 in.) and 2.5 c., (1 in.) and from the 2 c. (3/4 in.) distances raise perpendiculars to the first cross line.

5. Cut out along the thickened lines, and half or three parts through along the dotted line *ab*.

6. For the front of the pocket cut out an oblong of cardboard 25 c. x 5 c. (9 7/8 in. x 2 in.); from each end set off distances on the long sides of 4 ½ c. and 4 c. (1 ¾ in. and 1 5/8 in.) and join the points across the oblong by lines parallel to the ends. (Fig. 2).

7. Cut half or three parts through along dotted lines.

8. Bend base of pocket backwards from *ab* (Fig. 1) and from the half-cuts in Fig. 2, and fit the latter round the base of pocket. (Fig. 1).

9. Bind lines of juncture *ac, bd*.

10. Bind outside the base of the pocket.

11. Bind outside lines of half-cuts.

12. Bind upper edge of pocket front.

13. Bind the top edge of the back.

14. Punch small holes at *e* and *f*.

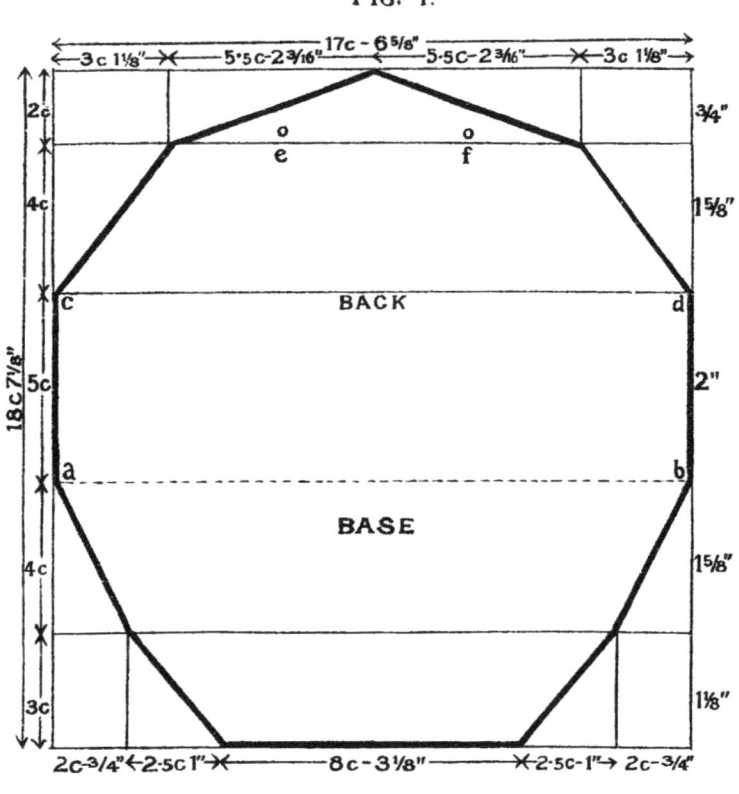

Fig. 1.

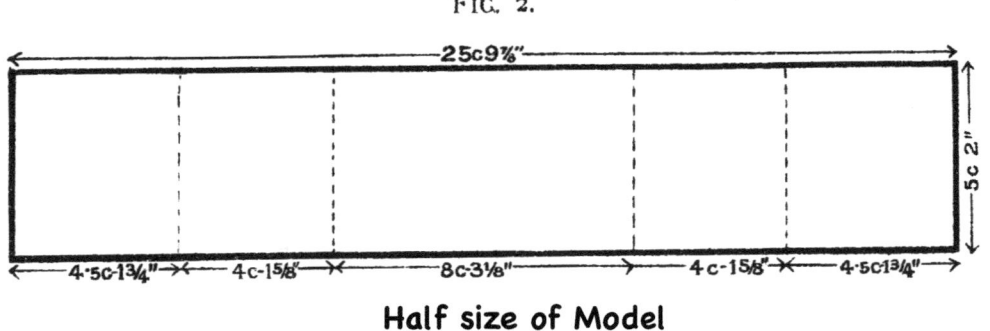

Fig. 2.

Half size of Model

MODEL No. 44

WALL POCKET—*with semi-circular front*

19 c. x 16.5 c. x 5 c. (7 ½ in. x 2 9/16 in. x 2 in.)

1. Describe an oblong 19 c. x 5 c. (7 ½ in. x 2 in.).
2. From *c*, the center of side *ab*, raise a perpendicular (*cd*) of 3 c. (1 3/16 in.) within the oblong.
3. With point *d* as center, and *da* or *db* as radius, describe the semicircle *aba*.
4. Cut out along the thickened lines, and half or three parts through along dotted line.
5. Punch small holes at *c* and *d*.
6. Cut out an oblong of cardboard 24.5 c. x 5 c. (9 5/8 in. x 2 in.) for the front.
7. Bend base of pocket backward from *ab*, and fit this oblong round the curve.
8. Bind ends of the oblong to the back of the pocket along the perpendicular joins.
9. Bind (i.) round lower curve, (ii.) round upper curve, (iii.) upper and lower edges of the back.

CARDBOARD MODELLING

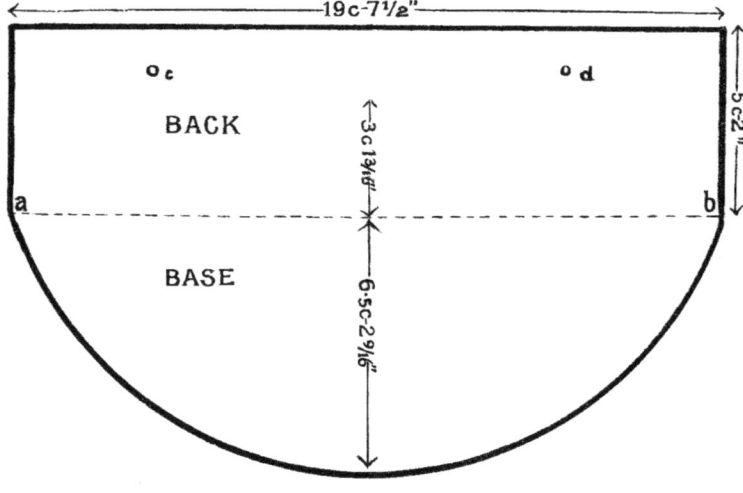

Half size of Model

MODEL No. 45

IRREGULAR OCTAGONAL TRAY

9 c. x 9 c. x 3 c. (3 ½ in. x 3 ½ in. x 1 3/16 in.)

1. Describe a square *ABCD*, sides 9 c. (3 ½ in.)

2. From each angle set off a distance along each side of 2.25 c. (7/8 in.).

3. Join the points thus found across the angle, forming an irregular octagon.

4. Describe a square of 15 c. (5 7/8 in.) having its sides parallel to the sides of *ABCD*, and distant 3 c. (1 3/16 in.).

5. Draw lines through the center of the squares, and the opposite angles of the octagon completed in Direction No. 3, and cutting the sides of the outer square.

6. Join these points across the angles, as in Direction No. 3, to form an outer octagon.

7. From each angle of this octagon, and along each side, set off a distance of 0.5 c. (3/16 in.).

8. Join the points thus found to the adjacent angles of the inner octagon.

9. Cut out along the darkened lines, and half or three parts through along the dotted lines.

10. Bend backwards from the half-cuts, and bind outside angles.

11. Bind inside angles, and upper edge.

12. Bind outside lines of half-cuts, and inside lower edge.

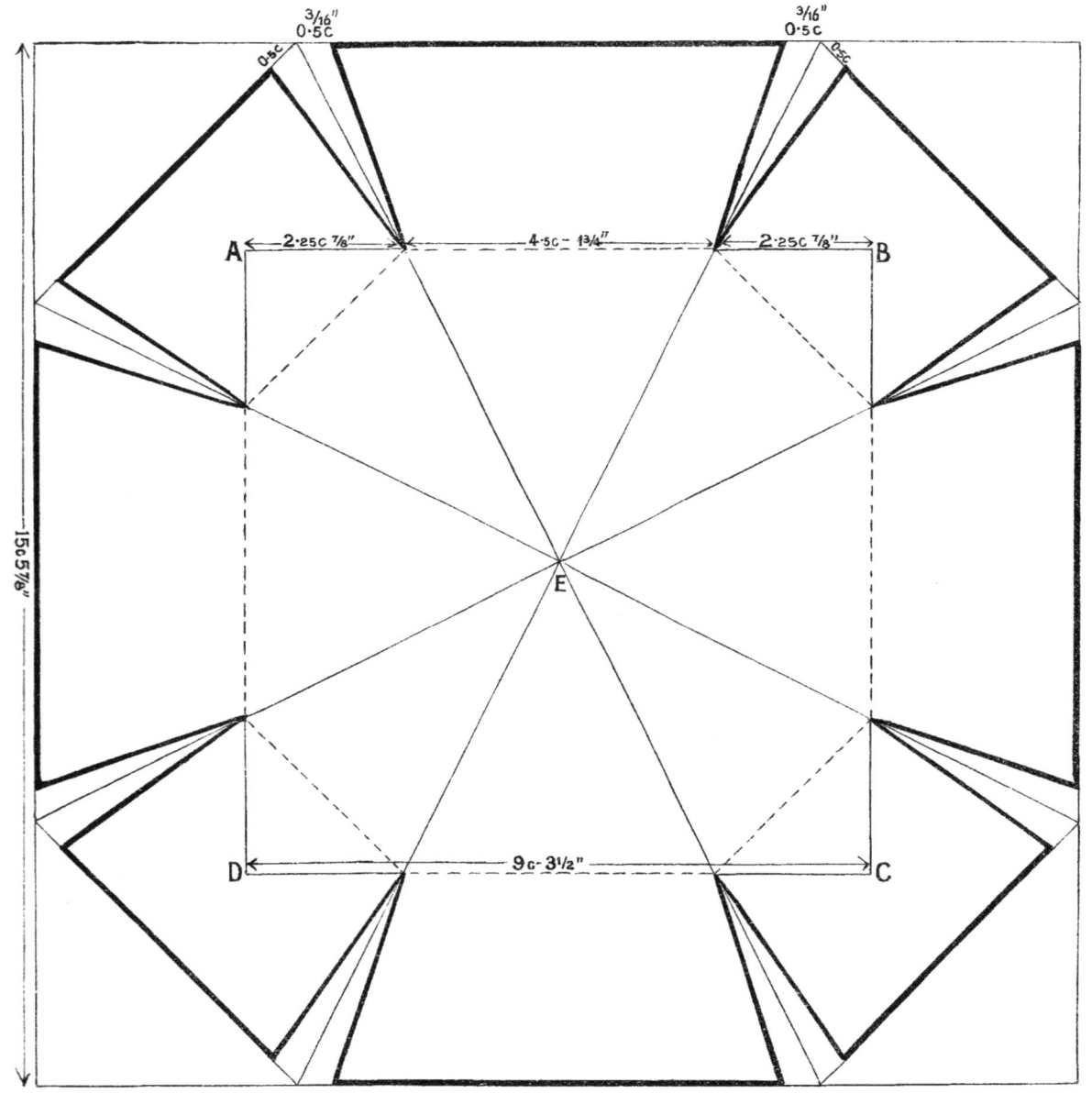

Size of Model

MODEL No. 46

IRREGULAR OCTAGONAL TRAY—*with curved upper edges*

9 c. x 9 c. x 3 c. (3 ½ in. x 3 ½ in. x 1 3/16 in.)

1. Describe a square *ABCD*, sides 9 c. (3 ½ in.).
2. From each angle set off distances of 2 ¼ c. (7/8 in.)
3. Join these points by lines across the angles, forming an irregular octagon.
4. Describe a square of 15 c. (5 7/8 in.) with its sides parallel to the sides of *ABCD*, and at a distance of 3 c. (1 3/16. in.)
5. Through the common center of the squares and the opposite angles of the octagon in *ABDC*, draw lines cutting the sides of the outer square.
6. Join these points across the angles as in Direction 3.
7. From each of these points set off a distance of 0.5 c. (3/16 in.) along each side of the outer octagon.
8. Join thee points with the adjacent angle of the inner octagon.
9. From each end of the long sides, with 9.5 c. (3 ¾ in.) radius, describe intersecting arcs; the point of intersection is the center for describing the curve of each long side.
10. From each end of the short sides, with 6.5 c. (2 9/16 in.) radius, describe intersecting arcs; the point of intersection is the center for describing the curve of each short side.
11. Cut out along the darkened lines, and half or three parts through along the dotted lines.
12. Bend backward from the half-cuts.
13. Bind (i.) outer angles, (ii.) inner angles, (iii.) upper edge, (iv.) outside half-cuts, (v.) inside lower edge.

Note: Bend binding while moist so as to fit along the curves.

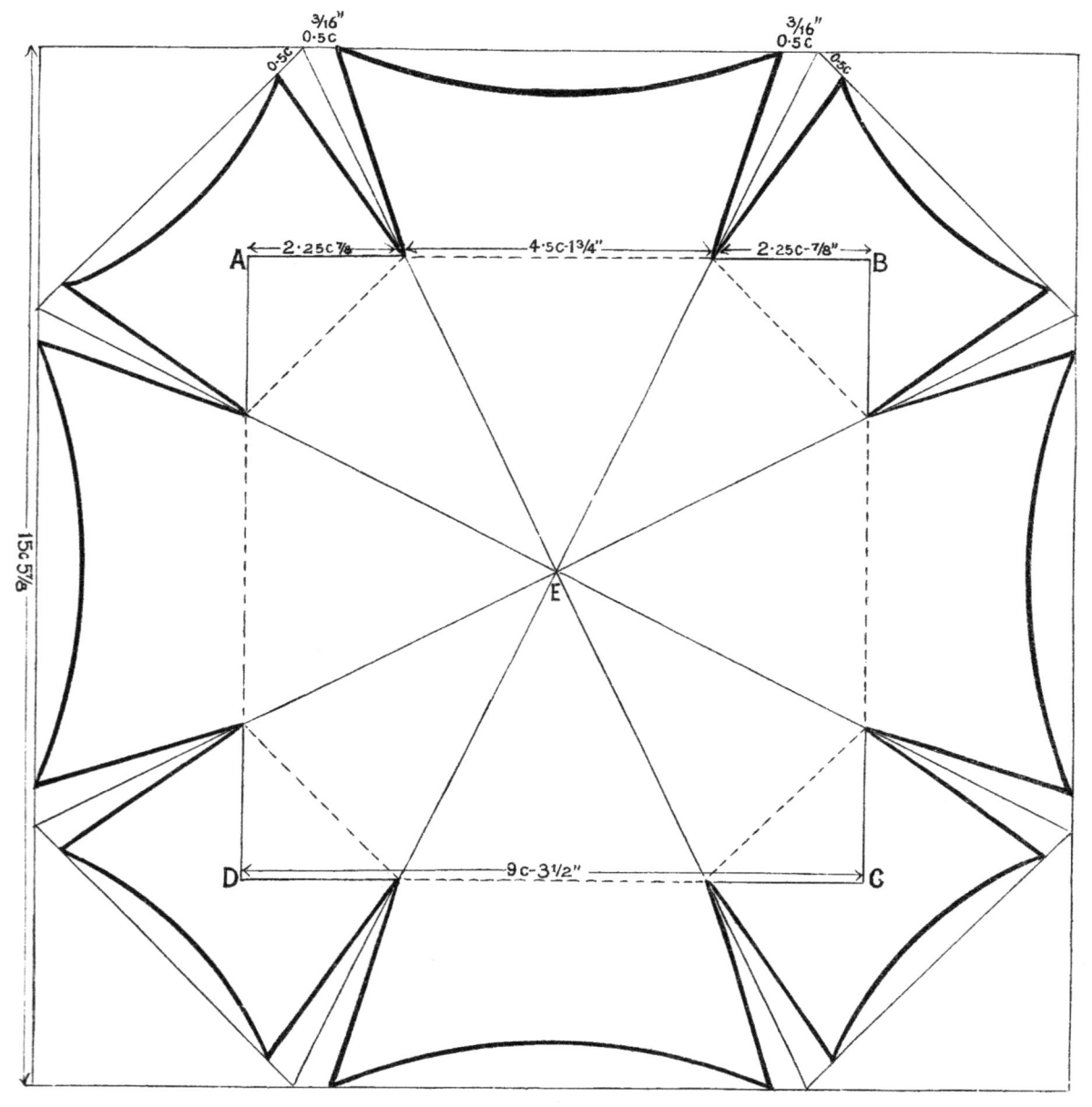

Size of Model

MODEL No. 47

OBLONG TRAY—*with curved edges*

18 c. x 8 c. x 3 c. (7 1/8 in. x 3 1/8 in. x 1 3/16 in.)

1. Describe an oblong 24 c. x 14 c. (9½ in. x 5 ¼ in.)

2. From each angle set off along each side distances of 3 c. (1 3/16 in.) Join these points across the oblong by lines parallel to the sides, forming inner oblong 18 c. x 8 c.

3. From each angle of the outer oblong set off a distance along each side of 1 c. (3/8 in.), and join these points by lines to the adjacent angles of the inner oblong.

4. At distances of 0.5 c. (3/16 in.) and 1 c. (3/8 in.) from each side, draw two lines parallel to each side.

5. Beginning at the 1 c. distance from the angle on each long side, set off distances each way of 3 c., 5 c., and 3 c., (1 3/16 in., 2 in., and 1 3/16 in.) as at *a,b,c*. Drop perpendicular lines from *a* to *a'* on first inner line, and from *c* to *c'* on second inner line.

6. Draw line with unbroken curves through a',*b*,c' from the 1 c. distance found in Direction 3.

7. From the 1 c. distance from the angle on each short side, set off distances of 2 c. (3/4 in.) as at *m, n, r*. Drop perpendicular lines from *m* to *m'* on first inner line, and from *r* to *r'* on second inner line, and draw curves as in Direction 6.

8. Cut out along the thickened lines, and half or three parts through along the dotted lines.

9. Bend backwards from the half-cuts, and bind the outer angles.

10. Bind in this order—(i.) inner angles, (ii.) upper curved edge, (iii.) outer lower edge along lines of half-cuts, (iv.) inner lower edge.

Note: Stretch the binding while moist so as to make it fit along the curves.

CARDBOARD MODELLING

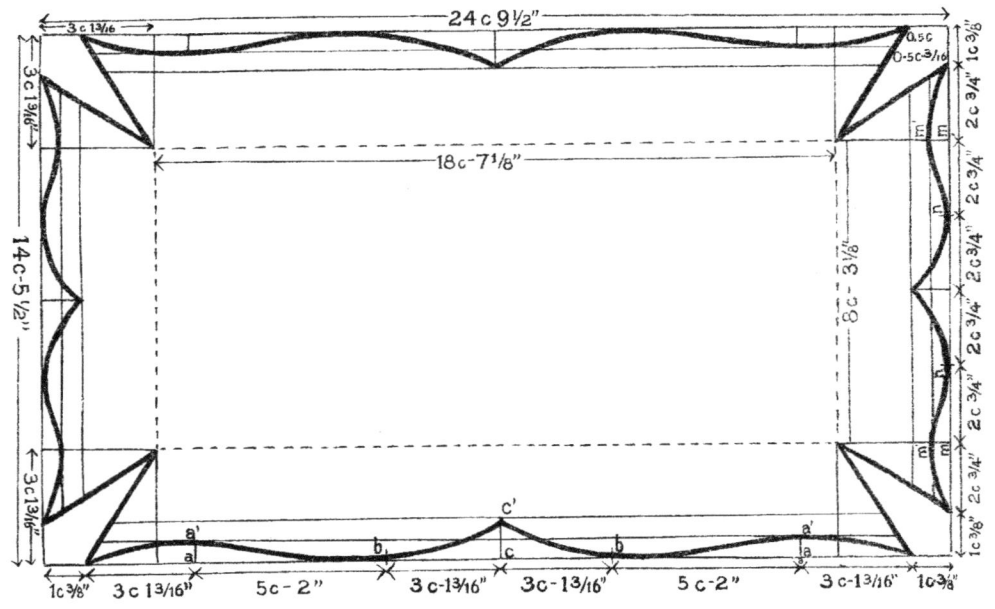

Half size of Model

MODEL No. 48

HANDKERCHIEF BOX—*with double and projecting base and lid*

15 c. x 15 c. x 7 c. (5 7/8 in. x 5 7/8 in. x 2 ¾ in.)

1. Describe square 29 c. (11 3/8 in.).

2. From the angles along each side set off distances of 7 c. (2 3/4 in.).

3. Draw lines across the square from these points parallel to sides.

4. Cut out along thickened lines, and half or three parts through along dotted lines.

5. Bend sides back from the half-cuts and bind outside perpendicular angles.

6. Bind upper edge, and outside lower edge.

7. Cut out two squares of cardboard, each 16 c x 16 c. (6 3/8 in. x 6 3/8 in.) and bind with 2 c. (3/4 in.) binding.

8. Fasten one of these squares to the bottom of the box so as to project 0.5 c. (3/16 in.) along each side.

9. Cut out a square of 15.5 c. (5 3/8 in.) and bind each side

10. Fasten this square to one side of box with a hinge of cloth 15 c. x 5 c. (5 7/8 in. x 2 in.) so as to form under part of lid. The hinge strip to go 2.5 c. (1 in.) along the inner face of the side of the box, and the same distance along the upper face of the square.

11. Fasten a restraining strip of cloth or ribbon from the upper face of the under lid at an angle along the inner face of the corresponding side of the box.

12. Fasten on the top of this under lid the remaining square obtained in Direction No. 7, and so as to project 0.5 c. (3/16 in.) from each side.

CARDBOARD MODELLING

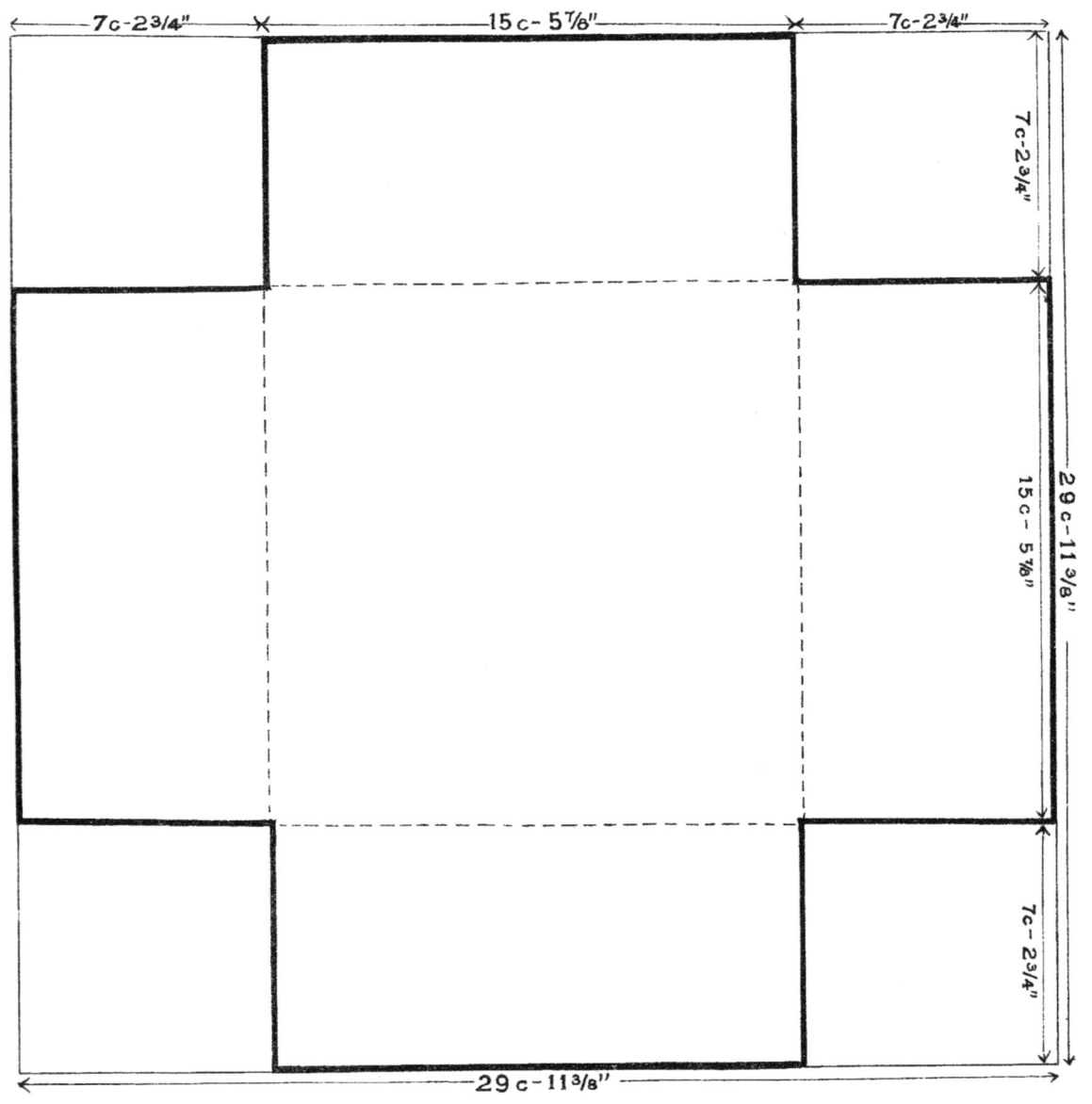

Half size of Model

MODEL No. 49

TOILET MIRROR—*with drawer*

DRAWER 14 c. x 9 c. x 3 C. (5 ½ in. x 3 ½ in. x 1 3/16 in.)

SLIDE 14 c. x 9.5 c. x 3.5 c. (5 ½ in. x 3 7/8 in. x 1 3/8 in.)

MIRROR 13 c. x 10 c. (5 1/8 in. x 4 in.)

For the drawer:

1. Describe an oblong (Fig. 1) 20 c. x 15 c. (7 7/8 in. x 5 7/8 in.).
2. Set off from each angle along each side a distance of 3 c. (1 3/16 in.), and join across oblong.
3. Cut out along thickened lines, and half or three parts through along dotted lines.
4. Bend sides backwards from the half-cuts, and fit at the corners.
5. Bind (i.) outside corners, (ii.) upper edge, (iii.) outside lower edge.
6. Cut out an oblong (Fig. 2) 9.5 c. x 3.5 c. (3 ¾ in. x 1 3/8 in.) and bind the edges.
. At A cut a 0.5 c. (3/16 in.) slit, and insert a folded strip of cloth, securing it firmly behind the board, and allowing strip to project about 1.5 c. (5/8 in.) in front.
8. Glue this oblong to one end of the drawer, so that the sides project evenly.

For the slide:

9. Describe an oblong 26 c. x 14 c. (10 ¼ in. x 5 ½ in.) (Fig. 3)
10. On each long side set off distances from the right of 9.5 c., 3.5 c., 9.5 c., 3.5 c. (3 ¾ in., 1 3/8 in., 3 ¾ in., 1 3/8 in.), and join across the oblong.
11. Cut out along the thick lines, and half or three parts through along the dotted lines.
12. Bend backwards from the half-cuts, and bind outside the line of juncture.
13. Bind outside the half-cuts. 14. Bind the ends.

For the mirror:

15. Cut out two oblong pieces of cardboard each 15 c x 10 c. (5 7/8 in. by 4 in.). (Fig. 4)
16. At *ab*, 4 c. (1 5/8 in.) from the end of one oblong, cut through the board.
17. Bind the piece A thus cut off, on all sides, except *a,b*., and B, on the two long sides and one short side.
18. Bind the remaining piece of each long side.
19. Join the small bound piece A to B by a 2 c. (3/4 in.) wide strip of cloth so that two bound sides touch when closed, and the ends of the strip overlap within.
20. For D cut a strip of board 10 c. x 1 c. (4 in. x 3/8 in.) and bind the ends.
21. Glue this piece into position D, and cover with cloth, 10 c. (4 in.) long, and covering 0.5 c. (3/16 in.) over the face of C, and 1.5 c. (5/8 in.) on the outer face of C.
22. Join oblongs B and C by a strip of cloth 3 c. (1 3/16 in.) wide, and 12 c. (4 ¾ in.) long, overlapping 1 c. (3/8 in.) within at each end, and leaving 1 c (3/8 in.) between the two oblongs.
23. Cover the inside of this hinge; join with a cloth strip 3 c. (1 3/16 in.) wide.
24. Take a mirror 13 c. x 10 c. (5 1/8 in. x 4 in.) and cover the back with black cloth.
25. Bind the edge of the mirror.
26. Glue the mirror to A along *cd* so that it lies on AB from *cd* to *ef*.
27. Glue this completed piece on the top of the slide from Direction 14.
28. Cut out an oblong piece of cardboard 15 c. x 10 c. (5 7/8 in. x 4 in.), bind the edges, and glue firmly to the underside of the slide, and projecting equally on all sides.

CARDBOARD MODELLING

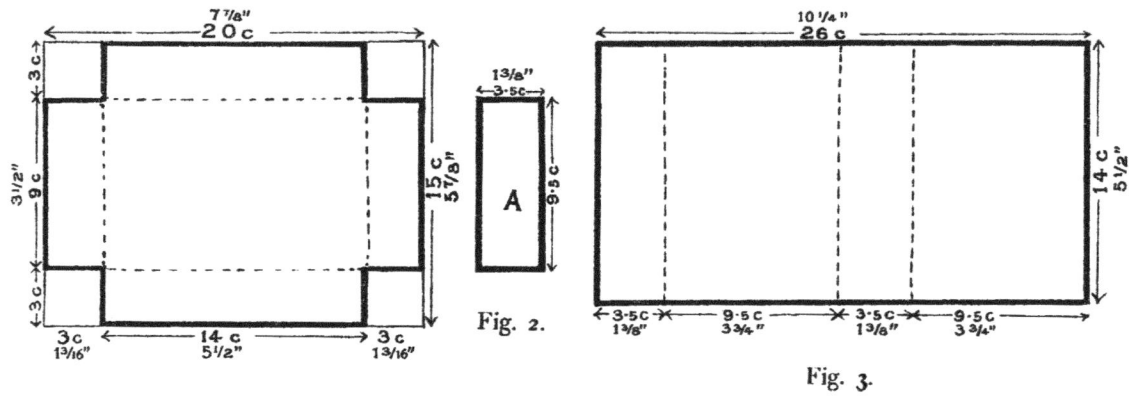

Fig. 1. Fig. 2. Fig. 3.

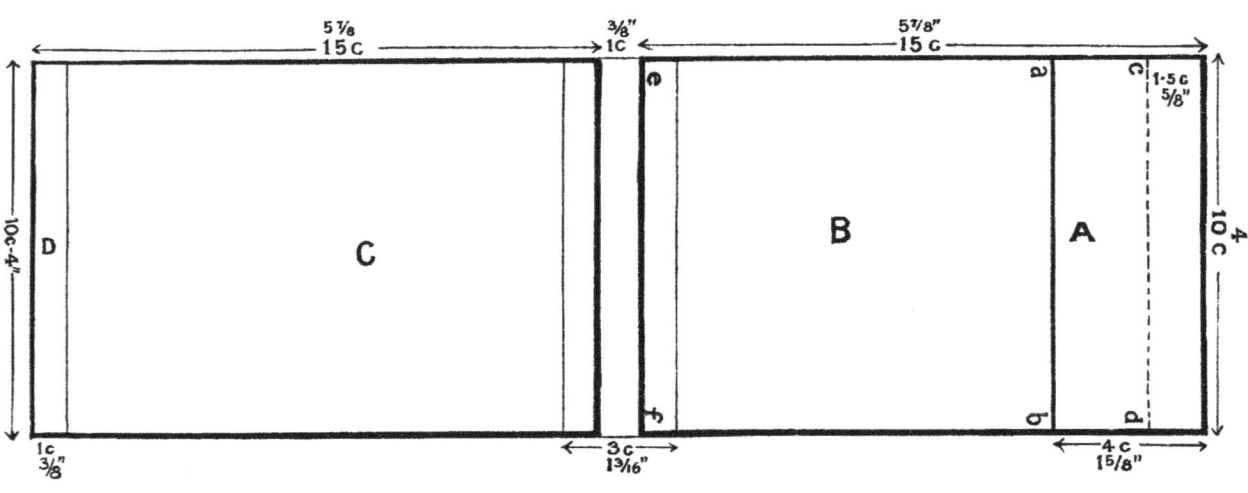

Fig. 4.

Half size of Model

MODEL No. 50

STATIONERY CABINET

16 c. x 14 c. x 6 c. (6 ¼ in. x 5 ½ in. x 2 3/8 in.)

1. Describe an oblong *ABCD* 28 c. x 27 c. (11 in. x 10 5/8 in.)
2. Along *AB* and *DC* set off from each angle a distance of 6 c. (2 3/8 in.).
3. From *A* and *B* set off along *AD, BC* distances of 7 c., 7 c., 6 c., (2 ¾ in., 2 ¾ in., 2 3/8 in.).
4. Join opposite points found in Directions 2 and 3 across the oblong.
5. From *a* and *b* set off towards the center of *AB* 1.5 c., (9/16 in.).
6. Set out as shown in drawing.

7. Divide the base into three equal strips. If metric measurements are used the strips will be 2 c. If English measure is used the equivalent of 2 c. in about ¾ in. The widths should be taken from the drawing.
8. Divide sides into similar strips.
9. Cut out along the thickened lines and half or three parts through along dotted lines.
10. Bend backwards from half-cuts, and fit so that *c, d, e,* and *f* meet *c', d', e'* and *f*.
11. Bind top edge *e, g, h, f,* and from edge *e', f'*.
12. Bind outside lines of junction.
13. Cut two oblongs to fit along fine lines of base and sides (i) 16 c. x 8.75 c. and (ii.) 16 c. x 10.5 c. (6 ¼ in. x 3 7/16 in. and 6 ¼ in. x 4 1/8 in.).
14. Bind one long side of each, and fix along fine lines with glue.
15. Cut narrow strips to fit against the sides of the cabinet and between the partitions fitted in Direction 14; bind top end of **each, and fix in place with glue.**

CARDBOARD MODELLING

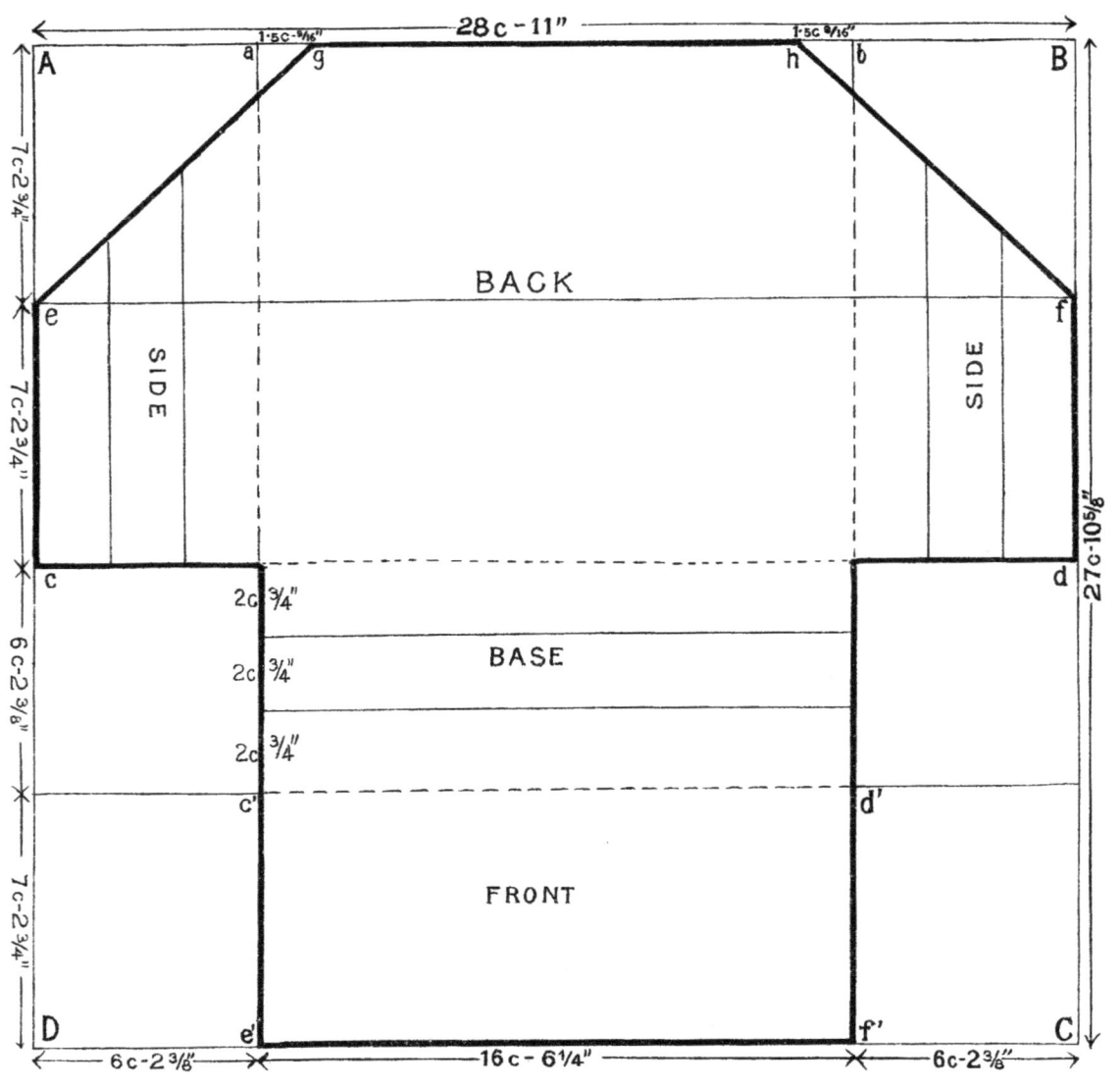

Half size of Model

MODEL No. 51

GLOVE BOX

28 c. x 8 c. x 3 c. (11 in. x 3 1/8 in. x 1 3/16 in.)

1. Describe an oblong 34 c. x 14 c. (13 3/8 in. x 5 ½ in.)
2. From each angle set off along each side distances of 3 c. (1 3/16 in.)
3. Join thee points across the oblong.
4. Cut out along the thick lines, and half or three parts through along the dotted lines.
5. Bend sides backwards from the half-cuts, and bind as in former models.
6. For lid describe a similar oblong, and set off distances from the angles of 2.5 c. (1 in.). Cut out as before.
7. At the center of each long side of lid cut out semicircular finger spaces 1.5 c. (5/8 in.) radius.
8. Bend backwards from the half-cuts, and bind.

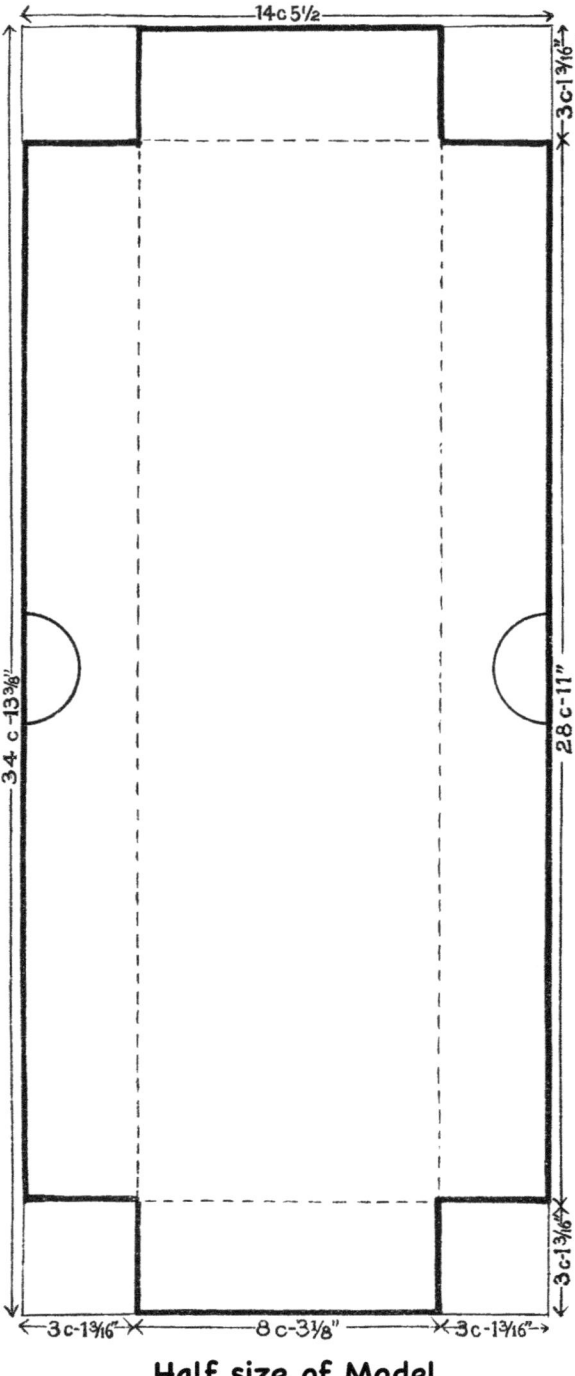

Half size of Model

MODEL No. 52

BOX—with hinge lid

16 c. x 10 c. x 7.5 c. (6 ¼ in. x 4 in. x 3 in.)

1. Describe an oblong 31 c. x 25 c. (12 ¼ in. x 10 in).

2. From each angle set off distances of 7.5 c. (3 in.).

3. Set out as in plan (Fig. 1). Cut out along thick lines and half or three parts through along the dotted lines.

4. Bind as in former models.

5. For the lid, describe an oblong 19 c. x 15.5 c. (7 ½ in. x 6 1/8 in.). (Fig. 2)

6. Set out, as in drawing, 2.5 c. (1 in.) from each long side, and from one end.

7. From these points draw lines parallel to the sides across the oblong.

8. At the end, *ab*, from each angle, set off 1 c. (3/8 in.) along each long side, and draw lines across the angles.

9. Cut out as before and bind.

10. With a strip of cloth 3 c. (1 1/8 in.) wide and 10 c. (4 in.) long, join the lid at end *ab* to side *ab* on the box.

CARDBOARD MODELLING

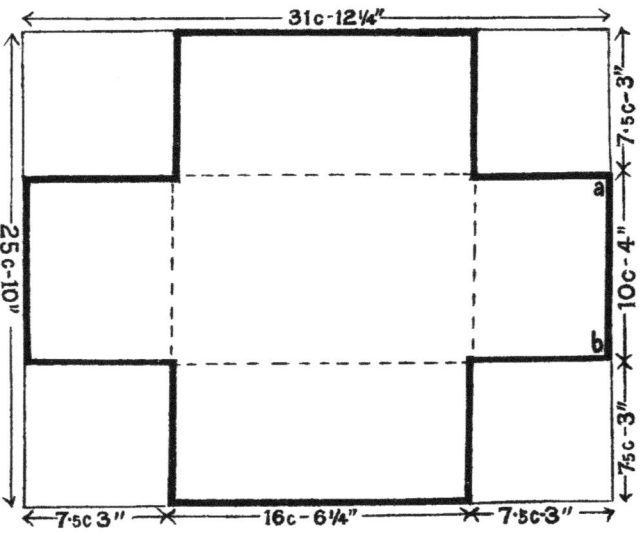

Fig. 1 (box)

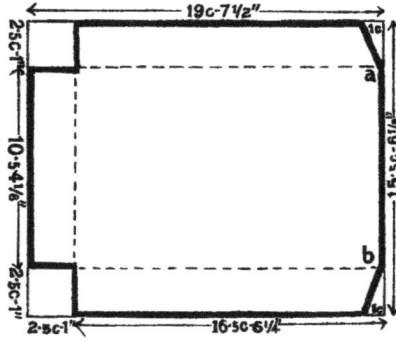

Fig. 2 (lid)

One Quarter size of Model

MODEL No. 53

TRIANGULAR TAPER HOLDER

16 c. x 9 c. x 7.5 c. (6 ¼ in. x 3 ½ in. x 3 in.)

1. Describe an isosceles triangle, base 9 c. (3 ½ in.) sides 7.5 c. (3 in.)

2. On the opposite side of the base, describe an isosceles triangle with 16 c. (6 ¼ in.) sides.

3. From the apex of this triangle as center, describe 11 c. (4 ½ in.) arcs.

4. From the ends of the 9 c. base as centers, describe 7 c. (2 ¾ in.) arcs, cutting the arcs described in Direction 3 at *a, a'*.

5. Join the points of intersection to the ends of the adjacent 16 c. sides, and to the ends of the 9 c. base.

6. Cut out along the thick lines and half or three parts through along dotted lines.

7. Bend sides backwards from the half-cuts so that *a, a'* meet.

8. Bind outside the joining line and lines of half-cuts.

9. Bind the edges.

CARDBOARD MODELLING

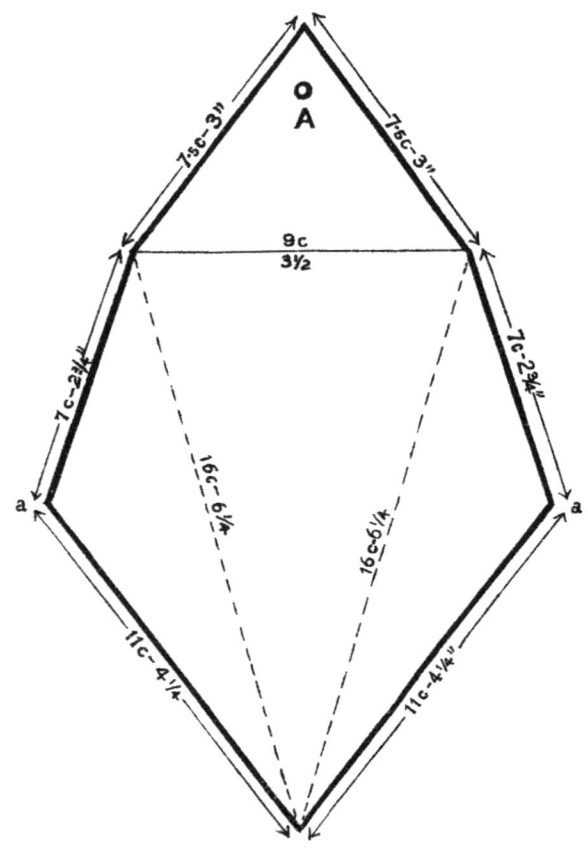

Half size of Model

MODEL No. 54

HANDKERCHIEF BOX—*with lid*

17 c. x 14 c. x 5 c. (6 5/8 in. x 5 ½ in. x 2 in.)

1. Describe an oblong 27 c. x 24 c. (10 5/8 in. x 9 ½ in.). (Fig. 1)

2. From each angle set off distances, along each side, of 5 c. (2 in.) and set out as in drawing.

3. Cut out and bind as in former models.

4. For the lid, set out, as in Fig. 2, with an oblong 23 c. x 20 c. (9 in. x 8 in.), and distances of 2.5 c. (1 in.) from each angle.

5. Cut out and bind.

Fig. 1

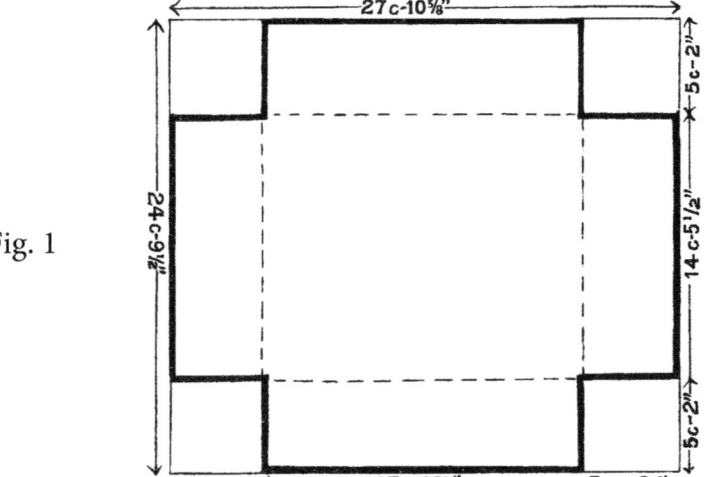

Fig. 2

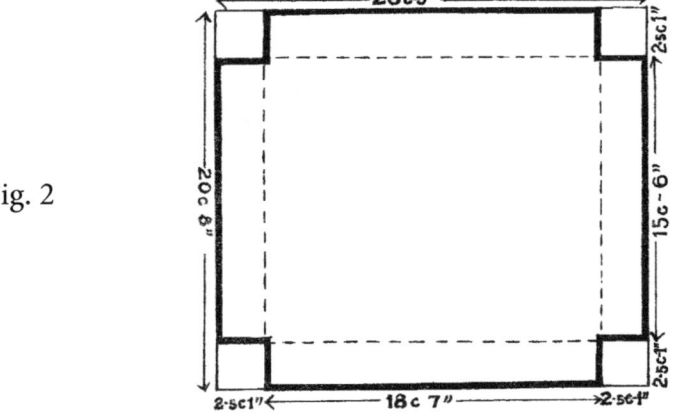

One Quarter size of Model

MODEL No. 55

STATIONERY BOX

20 c. x 12.5 c. x 6.5 c. (7 7/8 in. x 4 7/8 in. x 2 9/16 in.)

1. Describe an oblong (Fig. 1) 33 c. x 25.5 c. (13 in. x 10 in.).

2. From each angle set off along each side 6.5 c. (2 9/16 in.) and join these points across the oblong.

3. Cut out along the thickened lines, and half or three parts through along the dotted lines. Bend sides backwards and bind in usual order.

4. Cut out strip *A*, and bind its edges.

5. Join strip *A* to the edge from which it was cut, by a strip of cloth 3 c. (1 1/8 in.), so as to form a falling front.

6. For the lid describe an oblong (Fig. 2) 25.5 c. x 15.5 c. (10 in. x 6 1/8 in.).

7. Set out, as in the drawing, (Fig. 2) 2.5 c. (1 in.) from each angle. Draw lines across the oblong except on the *ab* side where lines are drawn across the angles 2.5 c. (1 in.) distant.

8. Cut out along the thickened lines, and half or three parts through along the dotted lines.

9. Bend sides of the lid backwards and bind angles.

10. Bind outside half-cuts, and cut edges.

11. Join the side *ab* (Fig. 2) to side *ab* (Fig. 1) by a 3 c. (1 1/8 in.) strip of cloth, leaving small space for the easy working of the hinge.

CARDBOARD MODELLING

Fig. 1

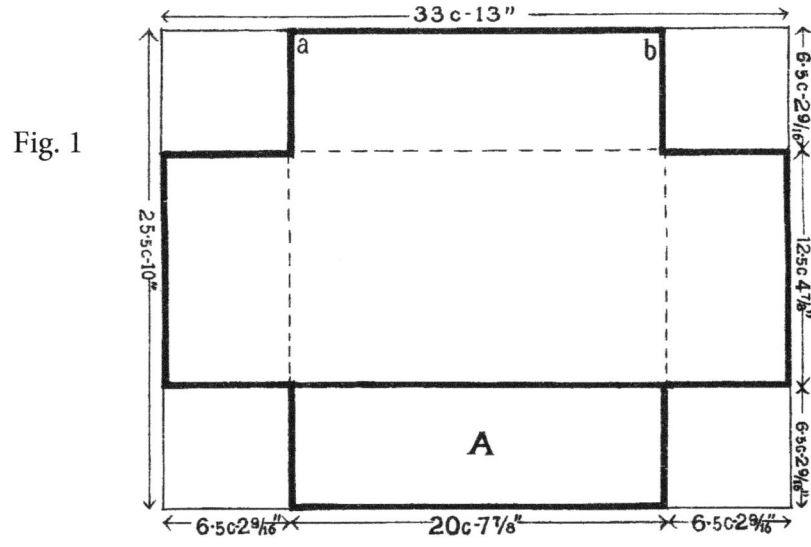

Fig. 2

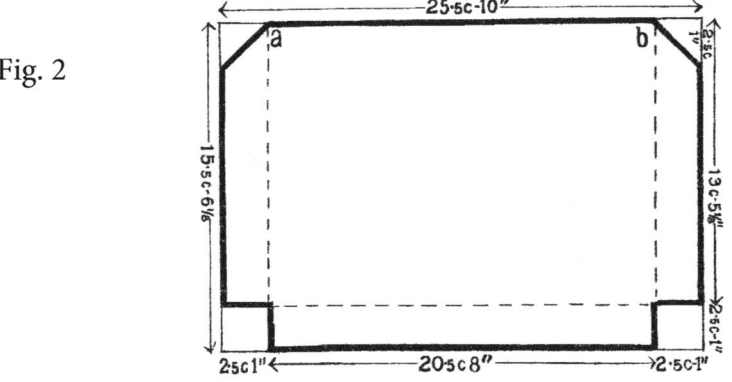

One Quarter size of Model

APPENDIX

Consisting of Drawings of Geometrical Models suitable for construction by Upper Classes, and for use in Model Drawing.

This appendix consists of geometrical drawings of models suitable for construction by children of upper standards, and by teachers for use in the model drawing lessons.

The flaps which are shown outside the dotted lines of half-cuts are intended for folding backwards over the lines of juncture and to be glued firmly down. These may, if preferred, be mostly disregarded, especially if the small models are being made, and the binding be performed, as in the *Manual*, by separate strips.

Sketches of the models are appended in order to give the pupil a clearer idea of the nature of the objects, and to facilitate their construction.

Definite measures are not given, these being left to the discretion of the teacher, and depend upon the character of the pupils and the purpose for which the completed models are intended.

If the work is being taken by children the objects should be small; *e.g.* in the first model the hexagons might have 1 ¼ in sides, and the prism be 3 ¾ in. long in proportion. If the objects are to be used as drawing models, much longer measures must be adopted. The proportional sizes of the different parts of each model are indicated by the drawings themselves.

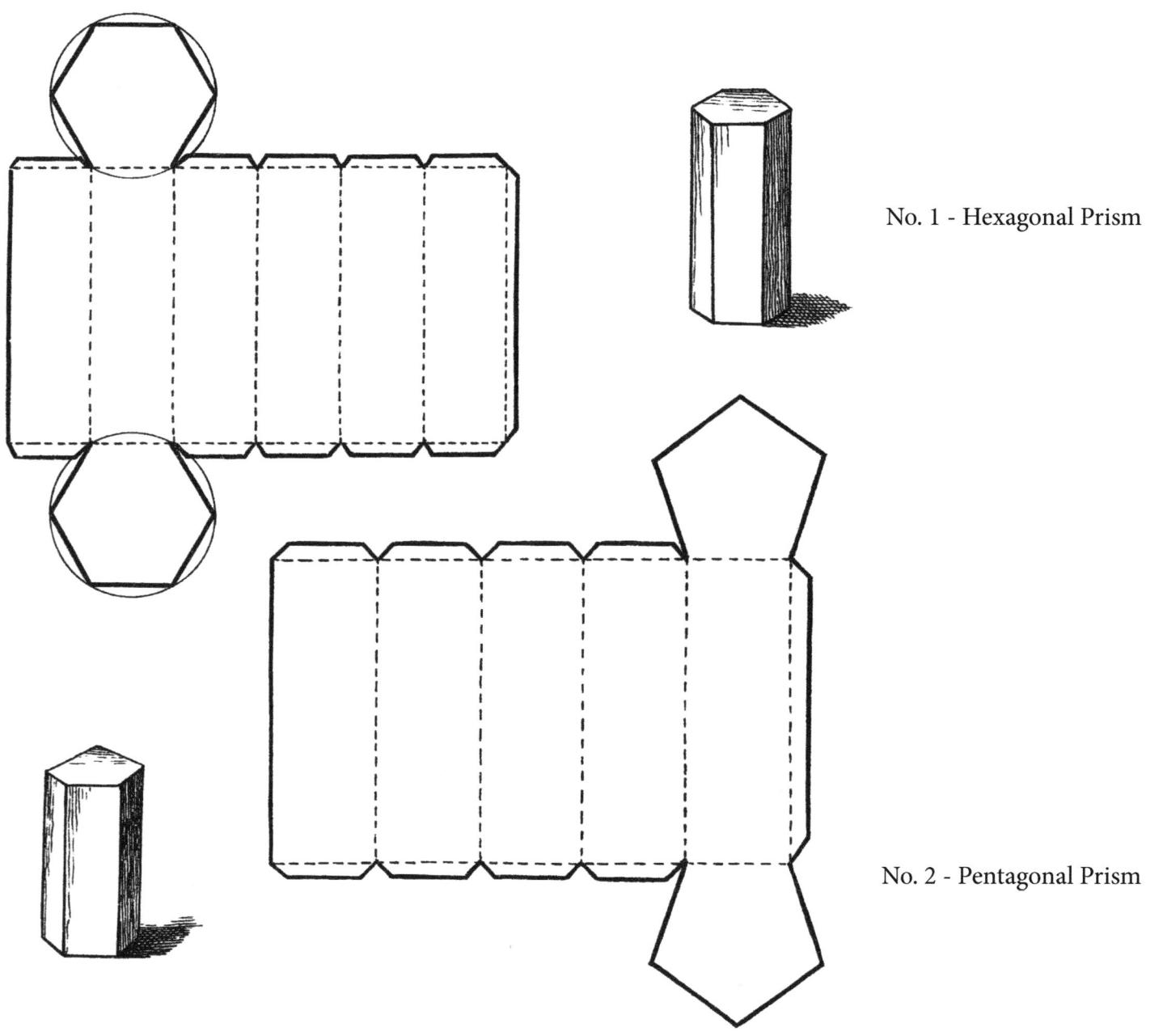

No. 1 - Hexagonal Prism

No. 2 - Pentagonal Prism

No. 3 - Triangular Pyramid with Equilateral Base

No. 4 - Rectangular Parallelopipedeon

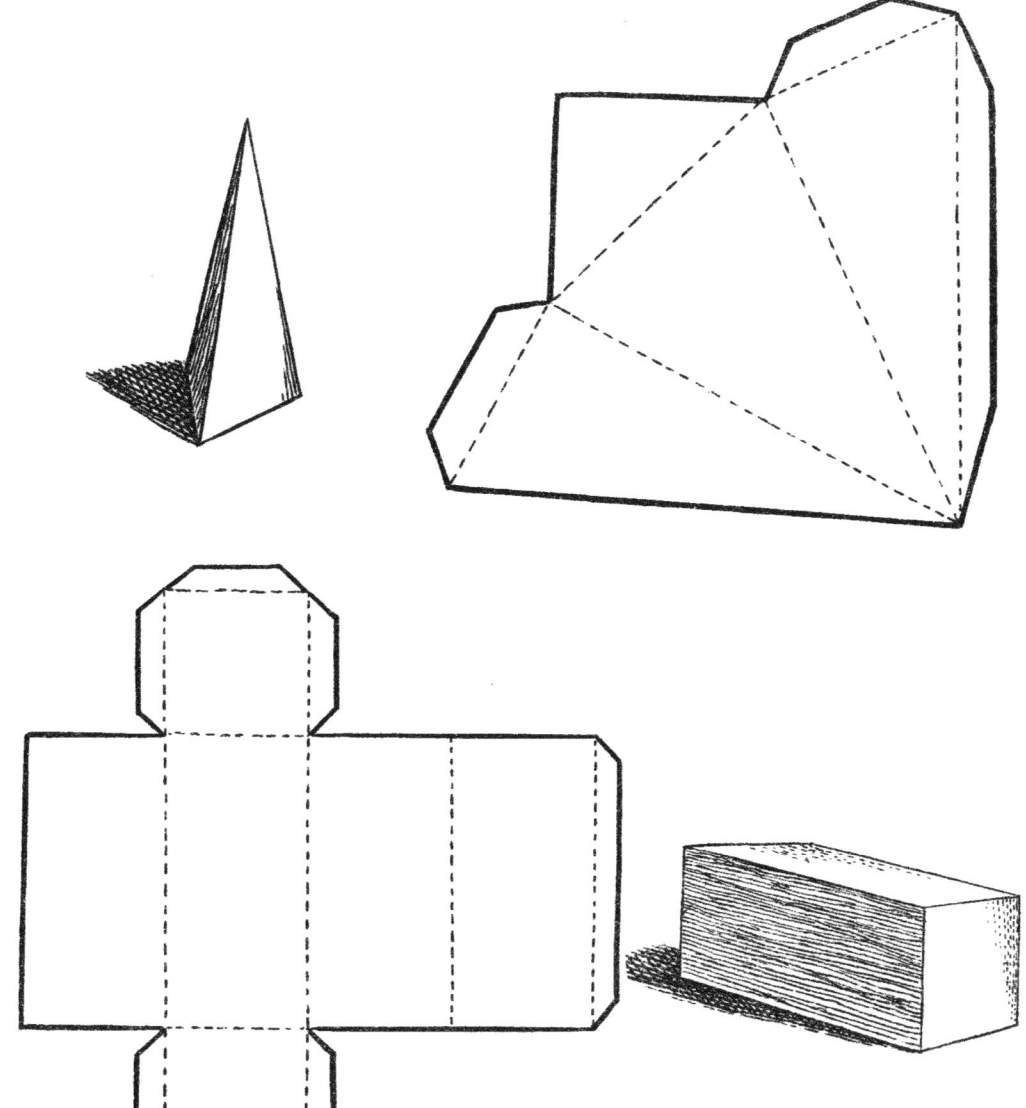

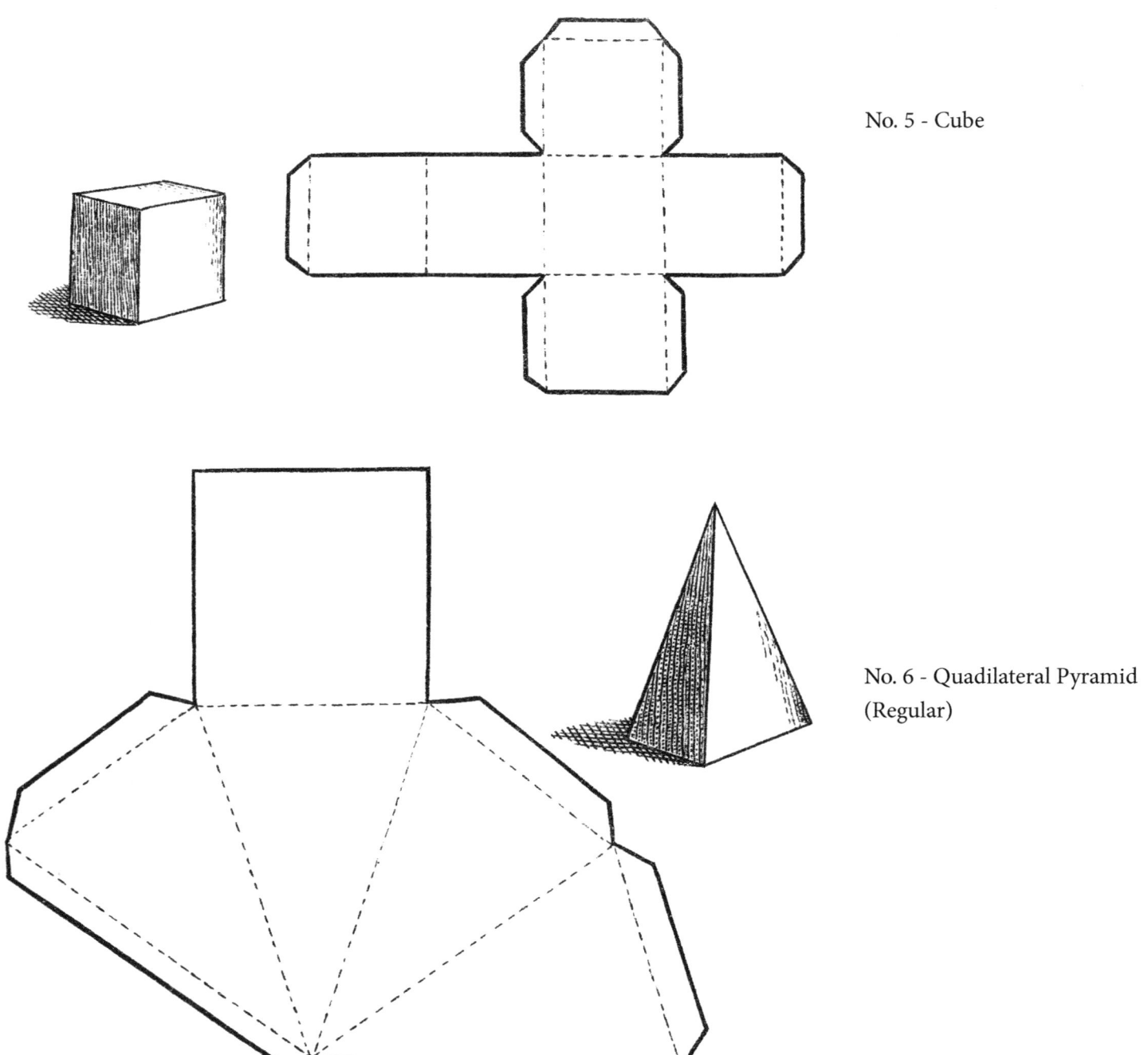

No. 5 - Cube

No. 6 - Quadilateral Pyramid (Regular)

153

No. 7 - Tetrahedron

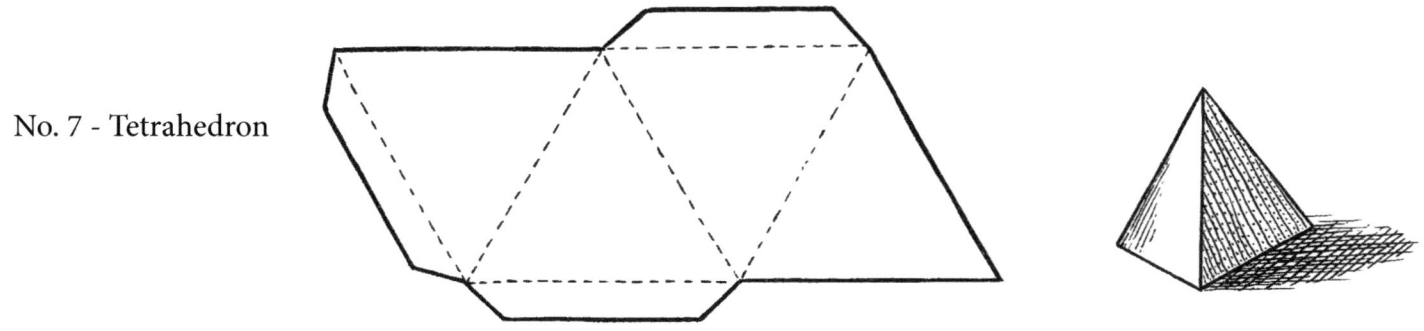

No. 8 - Equilateral Pyramid with Square Base

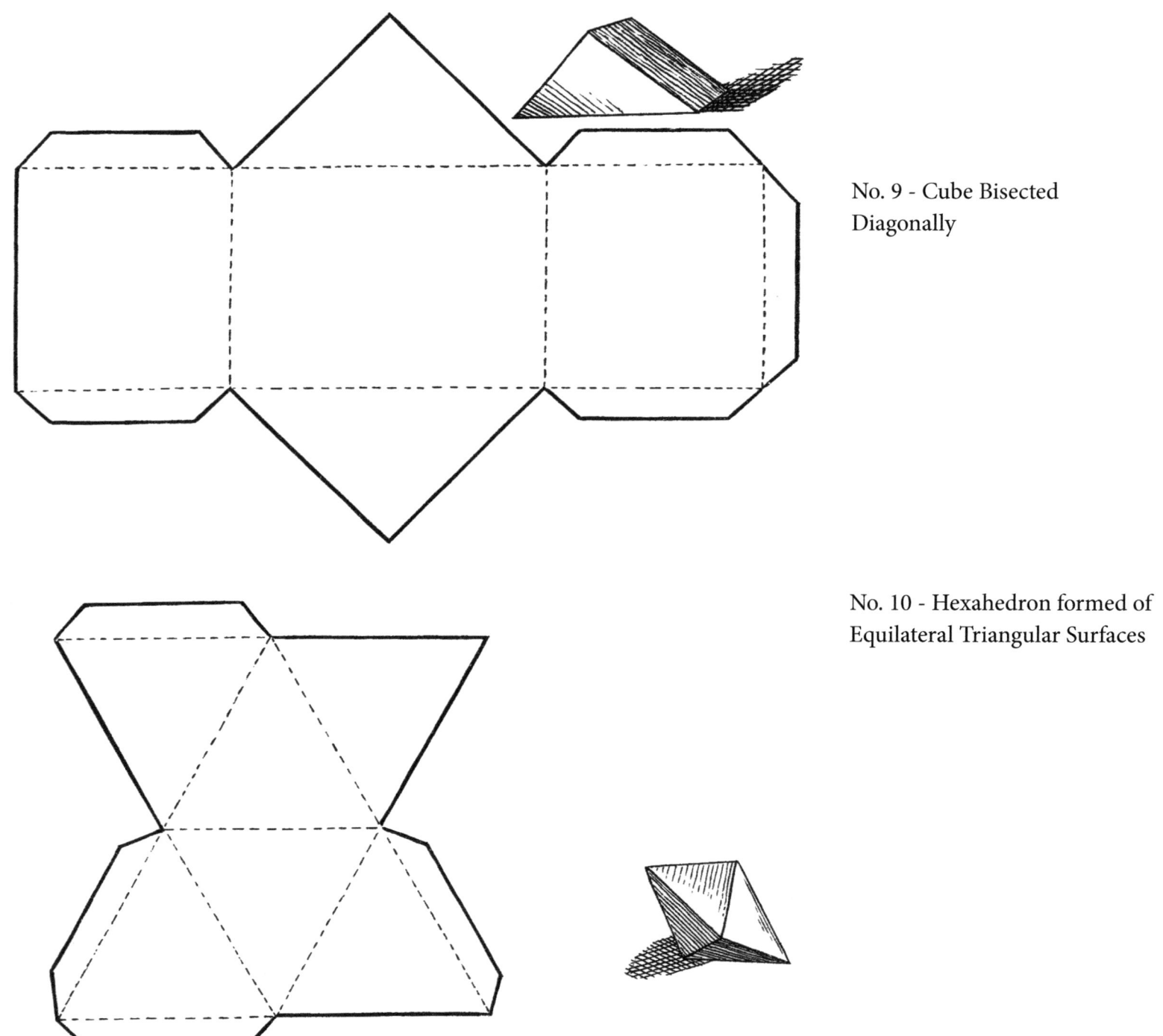

No. 9 - Cube Bisected Diagonally

No. 10 - Hexahedron formed of Equilateral Triangular Surfaces

No. 11 - Prism with Equilateral Base

No. 12 - Parallelopipedeon (Oblique)

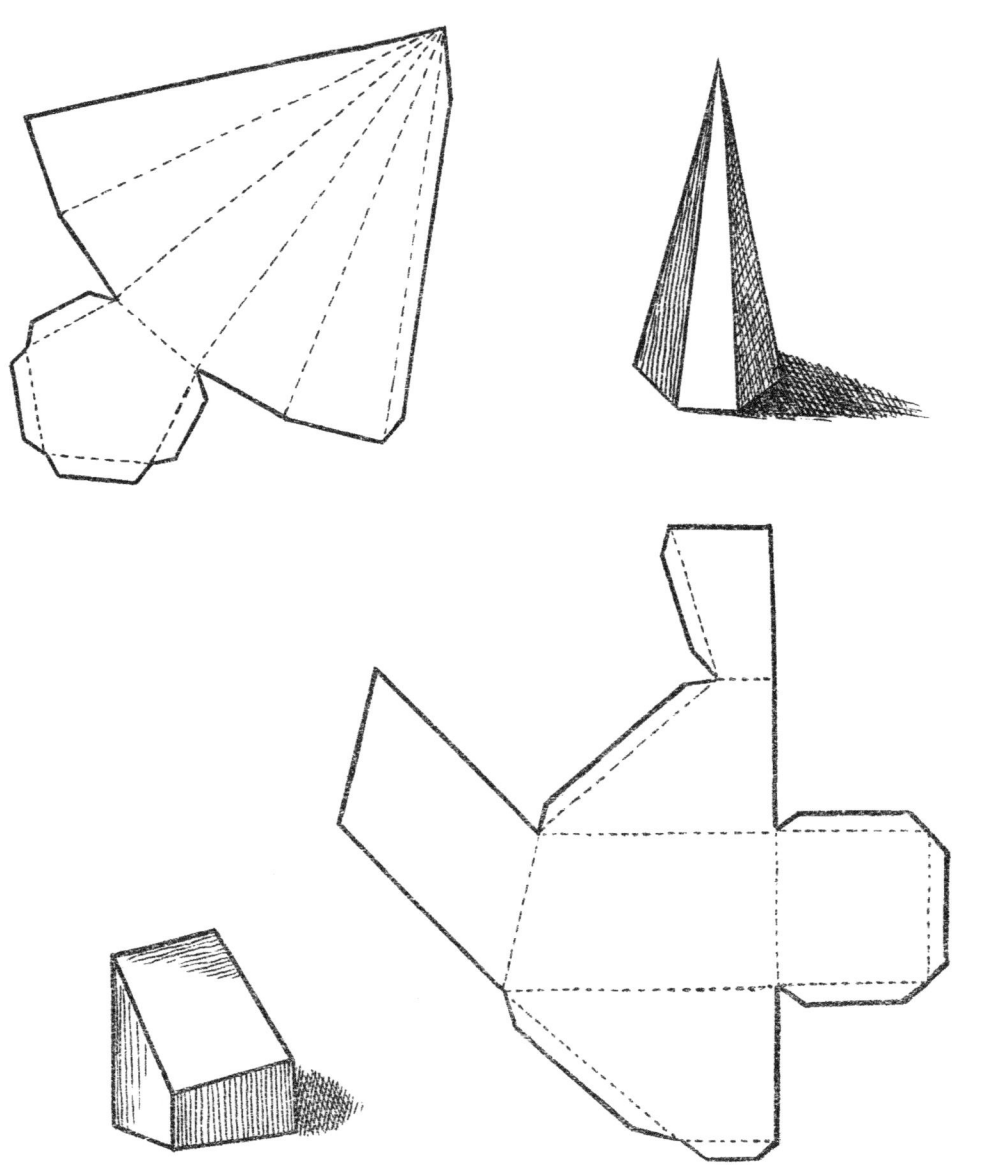

No. 13 - Pentagonal Pyramid

No. 14 - Irregular Quadilateral Prism

157

No. 15 - Seven-sided Pyramid (Truncated)

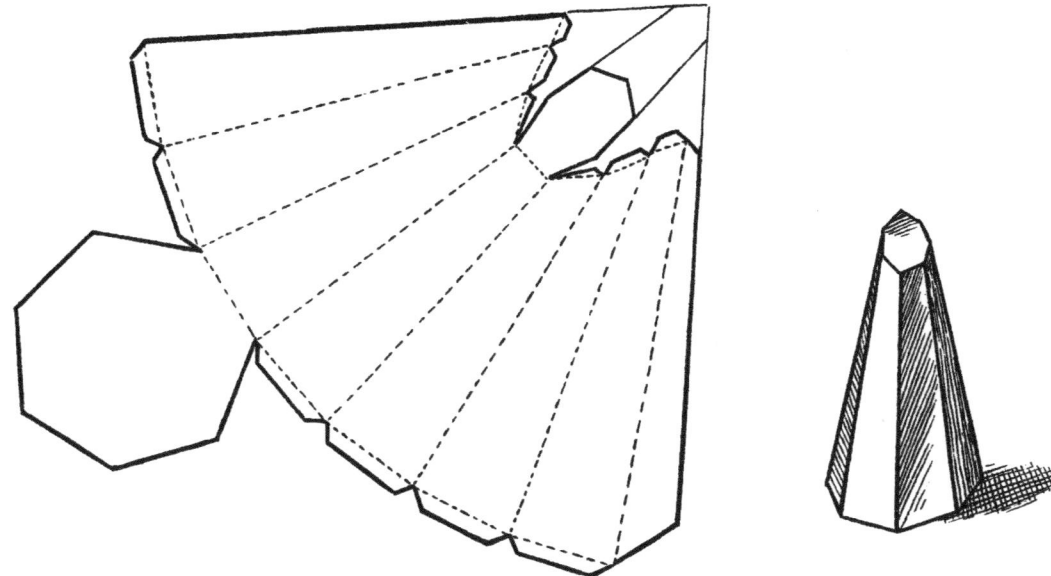

No. 16 - Irregular Quadilateral Prism with Oblique Base

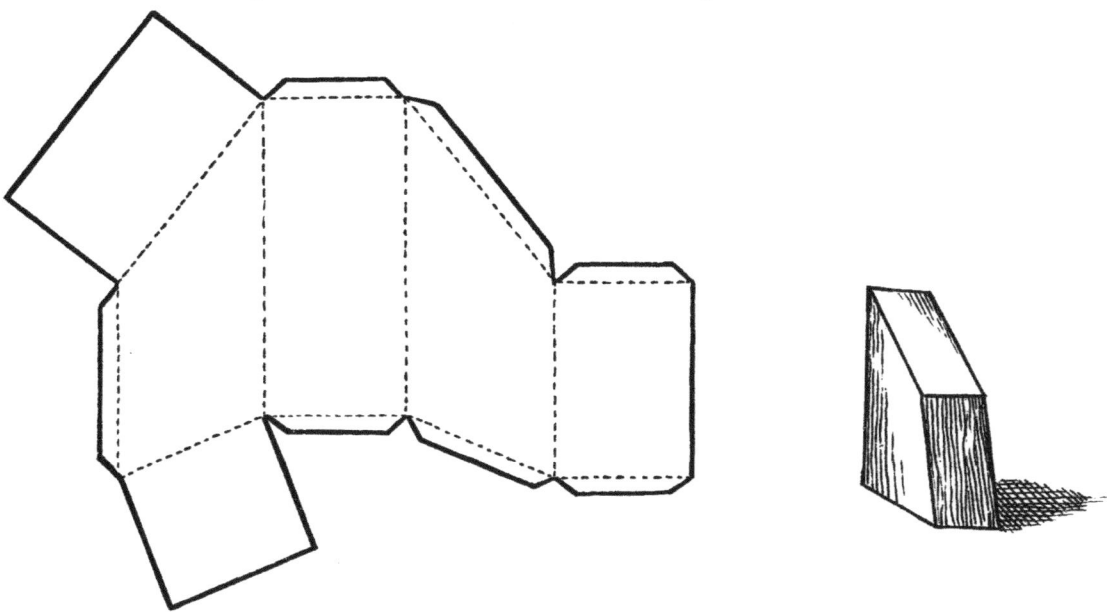

No. 17 - Trilateral Prism (Oblique)

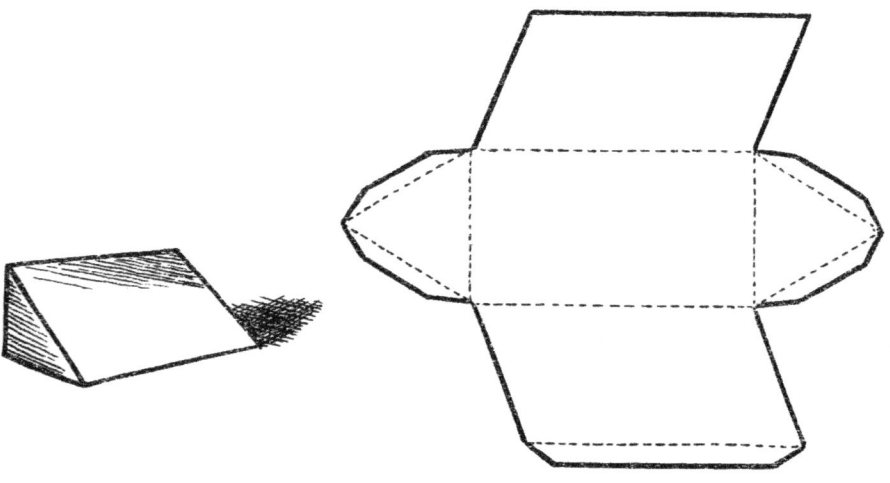

No. 18 - Quadilateral Prism (Oblique)

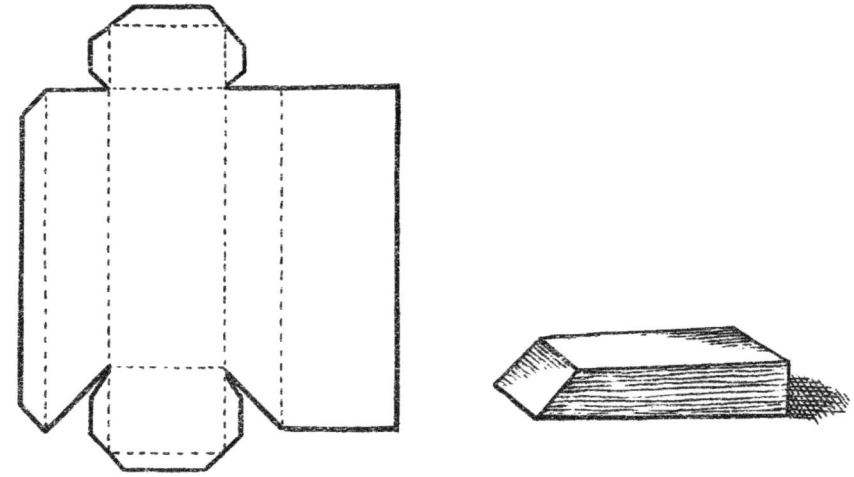

No. 19 - Regular Trilateral Prism (Oblique)

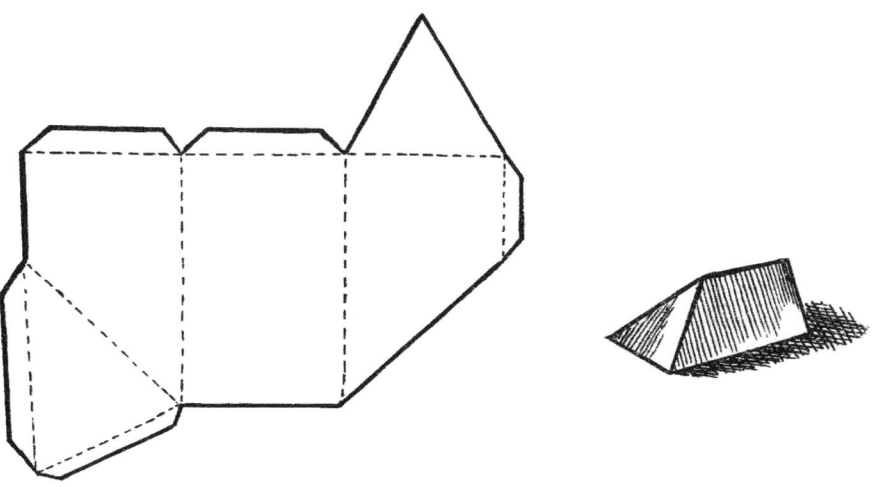

No. 20 - Icosahedron (20-sided Figure, each formed of Equilateral Triangular Surfaces)

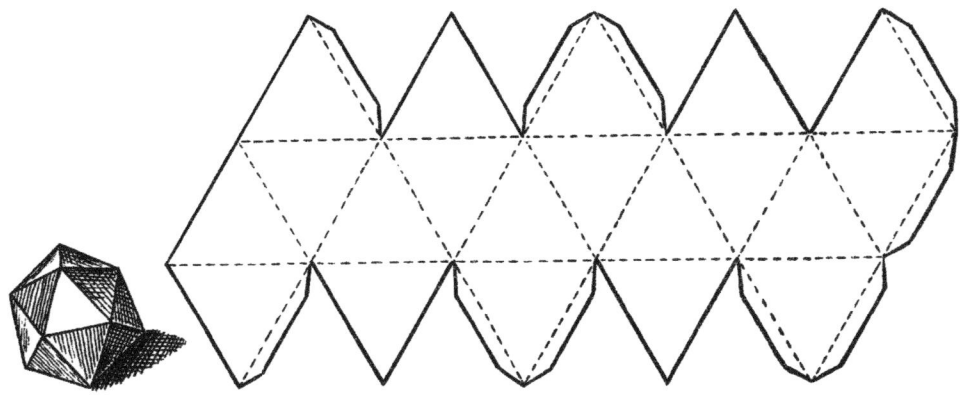

ADDENDA

Scale references apply to measurements of lines and not to areas.

*Editor's note - In the original volume, there were several errors listed that the reader was instructed to find and substitute the corrections into the specific models. The editor has made those corrections and eliminated the errors that were initially listed here.

www.ingramcontent.com/pod-product-compliance
Lightning Source LLC
Chambersburg PA
CBHW041421160426
42811CB00105B/1890